Custody Disputes

Custody Disputes

Evaluation and Intervention

Edited by
Ruth S. Parry
Elsa A. Broder
Elizabeth A.G. Schmitt
Elisabeth B. Saunders
Eric Hood
Custody Project
University of Toronto

Lexington Books
D.C. Heath and Company/Lexington, Massachusetts/Toronto

Library of Congress Cataloging-in-Publication Data
Main entry under title:

Custody disputes,

  Bibliography: p.
  Includes index.
  1. Custody of children—Canada. 2. Custody of
children—Canada—Psychological aspects. 3. Custody
of children—United States. 4. Custody of children—
United States—Psychological aspects. I. Parry, Ruth S.
KDZ160.C87   1986   346.7101'7   85–45573
ISBN 0–669–11975–X (alk. paper) 347.10617

Published simultaneously in Canada
Printed in the United States of America
International Standard Book Number: 0–669–11975–X
Library of Congress Catalog Card Number: 85–45573

The paper used in this publication meets the minimum requirements of
American National Standard for Information Sciences—Permanence of
Paper for Printed Library Materials, ANSI Z39.48–1984.

The last numbers on the right below indicate the number and date of printing.

10 9 8 7 6 5 4 3 2 1

95 94 93 92 91 89 88 87 86

*To the children and parents
from whom we learned so much*

Contents

Tables

Foreword

The rapid pace of societal change is demonstrated by the continually rising rates of divorce in all Western countries over the last half of this century. As divorce has become more common, the stigma associated with it has declined. The children of broken marriages no longer feel apologetic, defensive, and embarrassed. Indeed the opposite may now occur. Children have been known to tell quarreling parents that the two should go the route of divorce like the parents of their friends. Dissolution of the marriage, return to independence of the individual partners, and healthy development of the children can and is being accomplished, although not without pain and distress in the vast majority of cases. But the picture is not all rosy.

When divorce was rare, society's guidelines for who would have custody of children and how they should be supported were relatively simple; they were determined by moral judgment and presumption about child growth and development. The situation has become more complicated as the rights of children in these situations are increasingly recognized. More recently recognized are the rights and abilities of parents to continue parental functioning despite the fact that they no longer reside permanently with the child. This latter right indeed is being recognized by the courts with the use of the joint custody principle as the preferred arrangement for the child's future in some jurisdictions. Joint custody, which can work successfully with competent and motivated parents, represents a step of major significance in the evolution of postdivorce living arrangements.

In many of these joint custody situations, the partners agree between themselves and commission their lawyers to enact the arrangements. The role of the courts and others who review the welfare of the child in these joint custody situations may become rather perfunctory. The courts, however, continue to play a major role in cases where agreement between parents cannot be reached. These instances, where extreme brittleness and hostility characterize the formal termination of a relationship, also see the children used as pawns in the continuing battle to prove one partner superior in wisdom, power, or the capacity to parent. The welfare of the children becomes lost in the welter of petition and counterpetition. The children live in a continuing state of unhealthy uncertainty and insecurity. These cases place a disproportionate load on the court system and represent an area where mental health professionals and lawyers can work together for mutual benefit toward resolution.

It was to this group that the University of Toronto's Custody Project addressed itself. It was supported by the judiciary with court orders for cooperation from both sides. In return, the project has provided evaluation findings to both sides and to the court. The stage was set for dealing with the most difficult cases in the most constructive manner possible. The process detailed in this book is extensive and intensive and indeed may seem to delay the arrival at a decision; however, it should be understood that this is not only designed to develop a detailed basis for the recommendations but, by a deliberate process, to seek negotiated arrangements through the course of multiple contacts with the adults and children involved. The project members have tried to develop recommendations from the point of view of capacity of each parent and from the point of view of the children's desire, weighted for age, and they avoided a priori judgments that one solution was better than another. The basic philosophy was the preservation of constructive parent–child relationships, but the recommendations ran the gamut of the possible permutations, and since the project deals with the most contentious cases, it has been necessary at times to recommend such draconian measures as supervision or termination of access.

The role of the mental health professional is well outlined in this book, developed to utilize in the best way possible the knowledge of childrens' needs and welfare balanced against parents' rights and feelings of entitlement. The project members have worked as a support group for each other over a number of years as they struggled with seemingly unresolvable issues. By negotiating to present their findings to the court and to both sides, they avoided the pitting against each other of professionals who had assessed only one side of the situation and could appear to be hired guns. The group recognized that they could take the evaluation process only so far and that the final decision had to be made through the court process. The relative neutrality of position helped with the acceptance of recommendations and the alternatives being presented and discussed in order to assist the final decision maker. The distillate of this work and hard-won experience is succinctly given in this book as it presents the points of view relevant to intervention in this area. The Toronto group is to be commended for enunciating general principles that are applicable across jurisdictions and for sharing their experiences, successes, and failures in the always challenging and sometimes impossible situations that came their way.

It has been a pleasure to watch this group continue to grow and to have an involvement, albeit peripheral, in their activities. It is even more gratifying to see this experience of both successes and scars being made available to the field. Efforts to mitigate the destructive end of the separation and divorce continuum are commendable for the saving of time and money from futile legal disputes. By concentrating on constructive alternatives, the project has attempted to increase the coping skills of parents and to prevent some of the adverse effects of divorce on children.

The book details clinical experience and shows what can be done in this difficult area. This presents the challenge and opportunity for others to add their contributions toward optimal resolution of what can but need not be a destructive life predicament.

Quentin Rae-Grant, M.B., Ch.B., F.R.C.P.(C)., F.R.C.Psych.
Professor and Head, Division of Child Psychiatry
Professor and Chairman, Department of Behavioural Science,
University of Toronto

Acknowledgments

The Custody Project owes its existence to its founding fathers, Professor Quentin Rae-Grant, head of the Division of Child Psychiatry, University of Toronto, and Dean F.R. Lowy, Faculty of Medicine, University of Toronto. Professor V. Rakoff, chairman of the Department of Psychiatry, has been generous in his support. The clinical and research goals of the project were developed and carried out by the Custody Project members:

Harvey Armstrong, M.D., F.R.C.P.(C)

George Awad, M.D., F.R.C.P.(C)

Elsa Broder, M.D., F.R.C.P.(C)

Clive Chamberlain, M.D., D.Psych., F.R.C.P.(C)
  (project coordinator, 1976–1977)

Jeanette deLevie, B.A., B.Ed.
  (project administrator, 1979–present)

Eric Hood, M.B., Ch.B., F.R.C.P.(C)
  (project director, 1984–present)

Eva Kenyon, M.S.W., C.S.W.

Simon Kreindler, M.D., F.R.C.P.(C)

Sam Malcolmson, M.D., F.R.C.P.(C)

Ruth S. Parry, M.S.W., C.S.W.
  (project coordinator, 1977–1984)

Eleanor Patterson
  (project administrator, 1976–1979)

Jerome Pauker, Ph.D.

Elisabeth Saunders, Ed.D. (research psychologist)

Elisabeth A. Schmitt, M.D., F.R.C.P.(C)

Robert J. Simmons, M.D., F.R.C.P.(C)

Our legal colleagues in the firm of MacDonald and Ferrier have given generously of their knowledge and time so that the Custody Project members could gain a better understanding of the legal aspects of separation and divorce.

This book, authored by Custody Project members and our colleague, J.C. MacDonald, Q.C., as guest author, has depended heavily on the assistance of Cathy Linton, research technician, and the editorial assistance of Lynne Stott, Chris Wilson, and Cheryl Harding. The unstinting support in innumerable ways of our project administrator, Jeanette deLevie, has been invaluable. Financial assistance for preparation of the text for publication was generously provided by the Hospital for Sick Children Foundation.

The cases presented in the book are fictitious and do not describe actual individuals or families seen by Custody Project members.

Prologue

The Gerrards

James and Susan Gerrard met and married in Boston while Mrs. Gerrard was attending art school and Mr. Gerrard was establishing himself as a promising young industrial engineer. Sixteen years later, they were locked in a vicious battle over the custody of their four children: Janet, thirteen years old; Stephen, ten years old; Alice, eight years old; and Lisa, five years old.

Mr. Gerrard, an only child, was raised in a small community in Vermont. His parents were hard-working, practical people deeply committed to ensuring their son's academic and later career success.

Mrs. Gerrard, the middle of three daughters, was born in England but emigrated to Toronto, Canada, as a preschooler with her family. Her parents, both schoolteachers, achieved financial stability quickly. Intellectual and artistic activities were a major interest for the entire family. Mrs. Gerrard was able to meet their expectations academically but was rather more shy and dependent than her sisters. Her admission to art college in Boston was her first venture away from her family. She felt lonely and isolated until she met Mr. Gerrard in her second year. Her senior by six years, he appeared assured, gregarious, and supportive. Mr. Gerrard perceived her as attractive, bright, and creative and in need of his protection.

Although their marriage was initially opposed by their families on the basis of cultural and religious differences, this diminished in the face of Mr. and Mrs. Gerrard's obvious satisfaction in their marriage. Mr. Gerrard's career prospered, and Mrs. Gerrard completed her art training and was perceived as a young artist of note. The couple led an active social life, primarily with Mr. Gerrard's business colleagues.

Some months before the birth of their third child, Alice, Mrs. Gerrard became mildly depressed and went to Toronto with the older children for a visit with her family. She postponed her return to Boston *several times. Mr. Gerrard then made the decision to establish a consulting business in the Toronto area, and the family moved there shortly after Alice's birth.*

Mr. Gerrard's business built steadily but required long hours of work. The couple rarely could enjoy leisure activities together. Mrs. Gerrard's previous interest in painting waned.

In the eleventh year of marriage, their fourth child was born. Mr. Gerrard's business trips occurred more frequently and for longer periods of time. His socializing with business colleagues was more often outside the home, without his wife, her absence being explained by him as due to the demands of home and child care. Visitors to the Gerrards' home began to notice a growing listlessness in Mrs. Gerrard and an atmosphere of neglect in the care of the home.

Mrs. Gerrard, aware of the growing emotional distance between Mr. Gerrard and herself, his rare appearances in the home during the children's waking hours, and her own recurrent feelings of depression, sought Mr. Gerrard's agreement to seek marital counseling. He rejected this flatly, stating that she was lazy, spoiled, and overly dependent on her family and that the remedy lay in her "growing up" and undertaking the responsibilities of a wife and mother.

Mrs. Gerrard sought psychiatric assistance for herself but discontinued it when Mr. Gerrard refused to pay the fees. Unknown to one another, each sought legal advice but did nothing further.

Shortly after their carefully avoided fourteenth wedding anniversary, Mrs. Gerrard was served papers informing her that her husband had petitioned for divorce on grounds of mental cruelty. Within hours Mrs. Gerrard made a near-fatal suicide attempt. The children found her and sought neighbors' help in getting her to the hospital. A month later, Mrs. Gerrard counterpetitioned on grounds of adultery, citing an employee of Mr. Gerrard's as correspondent.

At the point of referral for custody and access evaluation, the Gerrards had for a year been cohabiting but separate and apart. Each had been advised to remain within the matrimonial home until by agreement or by court order the issues of division of property and assets, financial support, and the custody and access of the children could be settled. Mr. Gerrard established himself in the basement family room, returning each day as the children came home from school in order to supervise their homework. Mrs. Gerrard avoided this part of the home, remaining upstairs, waiting for the children to come for supper when Mr Gerrard deemed their homework satisfactorily completed. Mr. Gerrard would then leave the house and return briefly in late evening to check that the children were in bed.

The children had long been aware of their father's lack of involve-

ment in the home, their mother's apathy, and the separateness of their parents' lives. Janet and Stephen had learned how to get to their father's office in order to see him. On one such visit, they had learned of his relationship with Lynn, an employee long known to them. Indeed, she had asked them if they would not like to live with her and their father. They kept this knowledge from their mother but told Alice. All three older children agreed that Lisa was too young to be told. From that time, the children turned more and more to one another for understanding and comfort. Their isolation from their parents increased following an incident in which Janet was asked by her father to chat with his lawyer, this resulting in a document in which Janet was reported to have been highly critical of her mother.

During the year of separate and apart living, the hostile enmeshment of the family intensified, and all four children had greater difficulty coping at school, with friends, and at home. Janet turned to a new group of friends with whom she became involved in minor delinquencies and truanting. Stephen, with a history of learning difficulties despite his good intelligence, achieved markedly less well academically, became tense and anxious about the homework sessions with Mr. Gerrard, and had difficulty sleeping. Lisa, normally an active, engaging little girl, was demanding and irritable with her friends and attention seeking and disruptive at school. Alice, an extraordinarily perceptive youngster, became the family therapist, worrying about Janet's activities and flippant manner, comforting and encouraging Stephen, mothering Lisa, and trying to soften the intolerable tension between her parents when both were at home. Communication between Mr. and Mrs. Gerrard was confined to messages carried by Alice, or sometimes Lisa, letters from one another's attorneys, and bouts of verbal abuse shouted up and down the staircase connecting their separate domains.

In endless affidavits and lawyers' letters, the parents' positions were stated with graphic detail extensively documented in support. Mr. Gerrard wanted custody of all the children, describing his wife as irresponsible and incompetent as a mother. Because he perceived her influence as destructive, he wanted only severely limited access in the future between her and the children. Mrs. Gerrard also wanted custody of the children, citing her husband's lack of attention to them over most of their lives except for his overly harsh demands for scholastic achievement. She wanted regular and frequent access by him to the children, providing this was exclusive of any contact with his girlfriend. Both parents requested possession of the matrimonial home until the youngest child reached age sixteen. Mr. Gerrard was prepared to provide minimal financial support to Mrs. Gerrard for two years. Mrs. Gerrard's position regarding financial support for herself and the children was that they should continue to live at least as comfortably as they had previously, with additional costs to be met for home maintenance and recreation once Mr. Gerrard was no longer involved in the family.

The children's primary wish was to remain together regardless of which parent obtained custody. All wanted frequent contact with the absent parent. Janet vacillated as to which parent she wished to live with but was adamant in her refusal to have contact with her father's girlfriend. Stephen felt that his mother would need his help and was fearful of failing his father's expectations scholastically. Alice expressed a strong wish to remain with her mother, with whom she had always shared artistic interests. Lisa wanted both parents, openly stating her expectation that the interviewer's job was to "make us all happy again."

The Grants

Chris Grant and Ellen Grant met in tenth grade shortly before Mr. Grant dropped out of school. At ages eighteen and sixteen, they married; five months later, their only child, Bobby, was born.

Mr. Grant was the fourth of five boys in his family. He described his parents and brothers as affectionate, easygoing, and quick to stand up for one another, particularly if one of them got into trouble. He, like his older brothers, had been involved in some delinquent behavior, but in Mr. Grant's view, his parents' had "taken care of this," and he had learned that the answer lay in not getting caught.

Mrs. Grant was the youngest and only girl in her family. She was an afterthought, born several years after her brothers. She described herself as having been an obedient, shy little girl until she began to rebel in high school against her parents' strict upbringing. Their expectations with regard to helping at home and high academic performance and their prohibition against dating until she was eighteen years old appeared to her as much more rigid and old-fashioned than those of her girlfriends' parents.

When Mr. and Mrs. Grant met, she perceived him as popular, handsome, and full of self-confidence. Mr. Grant enjoyed her admiring attitude toward him. They dated secretly at first. Following one serious quarrel with her parents, Mrs. Grant, then age fifteen, ran from her parents' home to Mr. Grant's parents' home. They welcomed her warmly and said that she could live with them. Within hours Mrs. Grant's parents arrived and demanded that she return home with them immediately, threatening legal action against Mr. Grant if she refused. Mr. and Mrs. Grant then planned that she would become pregnant in order to force her parents to agree to their marriage.

The marriage was beset with problems from the beginning. Each partner held expectations of the other that were not met. Mr. Grant had difficulty getting a job and spent much of his time with his male friends, leaving Mrs. Grant to the care of his family, with whom the couple were living. Mrs. Grant was uncomfortable in her in-law's home, alienated from her own parents, and frightened about her pregnancy.

At the time of Bobby's birth, Mrs. Grant's parents gave her considerable support and offered to assist the young couple in obtaining their own apartment. Both Mr. and Mrs. Grant reported the following several months as the most satisfactory of the marriage. When Bobby was a year old, Mr. Grant was laid off his job. He did little to find employment and again spent increasing time with his friends drinking. At home he was irritable and demanding, occasionally physically abusive to Mrs. Grant, and verbally threatening to Bobby. Six months later Mrs. Grant obtained a job and arranged for Bobby to be cared for by her parents while she worked. As her job success and financial security improved, Mr. Grant's alcohol and drug abuse increased; chronic quarreling with more frequent physical abuse of Mrs. Grant by Mr. Grant ensued. When Bobby was three years old and after a particularly bad fight, Mrs. Grant left her husband and sought refuge at her parents' home for Bobby and herself.

At that point both Mr. and Mrs. Grant recognized that the marriage was at an end. Mr. Grant agreed that Bobby should remain in his wife's custody, with her parents continuing to provide day care. He wanted frequent access visits with Bobby, these to be at his parents' home, to which he had moved immediately after Mrs. Grant left him. Mrs. Grant recognized that Bobby was very attached to his father and agreed to twice-weekly visits on the basis that Bobby's physical care and safety would be assured by the presence of Mr. Grant's parents. This plan continued without difficulty until Bobby was five years old.

During this two-year period, Mr. Grant's life stabilized considerably. In the second year, he completed a welder's course and held a job in which he achieved well. Mrs. Grant was promoted twice and was financially able to move to a separate apartment with Bobby, close to her parents' home so that Bobby's after-school care could continue to be at their home.

When Bobby was five and a half, Mr. Grant left his parents' home to live with his girlfriend. The access visits then occurred in their apartment. Although apprehensive about this, Mrs. Grant raised no questions, feeling that Mr. Grant had demonstrated an increasingly affectionate and responsible attitude toward Bobby. Three months later, after each of two successive visits, Bobby complained that he did not like visiting his father anymore: no one cooked any meals, his dad was always busy with lots of people having a party, and he did not want to play with Bobby. Two attempts by Mrs. Grant to discuss these visits were avoided by Mr. Grant, his girlfriend on the second occasion angrily telling Mrs. Grant to "stay out of their business." After one further visit described by Bobby as even worse for him, Mrs. Grant told Mr. Grant that further visits would have to be at his parents' home. Three days later, Mr. Grant picked Bobby up from school and disappeared. Two weeks later, Bobby was located staying with his father at the home of a friend.

Mrs. Grant sought legal advice and applied to the court for denial of access by Mr. Grant to Bobby.

Custody Disputes

1

Introduction

Ruth S. Parry

Demographically the Gerrards and Grants differ somewhat from one another or other separating and divorcing families. In their pain, they are typical of families unable to find for themselves a means of ending a former way of life. Parental direction founders in bitterness; the parent–child relationships are tenuous, colored by each family member's awareness of the potential for taking sides. Caught in a quagmire of indecision, resolution must await the intervention of an external resource: the courts, lawyers, or, more recently, the mental health professional. As Weiss (1979a, p. 207) stated:

> Separating spouses may be angry with each other not only because they blame each other for their distress but also because of genuine conflicts of interest. Such conflicts are most likely to occur in relation to property division, support payments, custody of the children, and visitation [access].

In 1971, the Honourable Mr. Justice Edson Haines of the Supreme Court of Ontario identified a need for clinical services for an increasing number of families appearing before him in contested custody and access proceedings. The need was two-fold: amelioration of the distress of the family members and assistance to the court in adjudicating the disputes through the availability of information about the parents and the children, which required the expertise of a clinician to obtain.

In response to this request, the head of the Division of Child Psychiatry of the Department of Psychiatry of the University of Toronto undertook to facilitate referrals to members of the faculty. All members were involved in a teaching center within the Child and Adolescent Division; all were familiar with the sequellae of acrimonious family breakdown as manifested by their child and adult patients. Under the sponsorship of the Department of Psychiatry, an association of colleagues working as private practitioners was formed as the Custody Project. The evolution of this group and its model for intervention are described in chapters 4 and 6.

In conjunction with the provision of clinical services to families, the Custody Project members set two further goals: the development of clinical guidelines for working with separating and divorcing families, an area of practice relatively new to most mental health professionals, and the development of knowledge about separating and divorcing families through clinical research. This book presents the views of the authors, members of the Custody Project, based in clinical experience and research findings. These derive from information and observations at some point of decision making as to the ways in which families dissolve their previous life-style and reorganize. Brown (1976, p. 400) has described the divorcing process as one with two major phases:

> The *decision-making* period begins with the consideration of divorce as an option, and ends with a decision to divorce which is implemented by physical separation. The *restructuring phase* starts at the time of physical separation and ends when the massive and rapid change is over and a relatively stable and autonomous life style has been established.

According to Brown, the restructuring phase comprises five major subprocesses, operating more or less simultaneously: the legal divorce, economic readjustment, restructuring of the parent–child relationship, social readjustment, and, most important, the emotional or psychological subprocess.

In the United States, divorce law varies among states. State divorce laws are increasingly drafted on the basis of a no-fault concept. In many states, divorce is obtainable if not contested in a year or less. The Divorce Act R.S.C. 1970, Ch.D-8 is the Canadian federal law providing five grounds for divorce. The no-fault grounds (section 4, subsections 1 and 2) is preferred by most couples. It allows for divorce on the basis of marital breakdown after a three-year separation. Brown's latter four processes in the restructuring phase of the divorce process cannot be held in limbo for three years pending legal divorce. Thus, for Canadian families, these processes tend to precede the legal divorce. Ontario's Children's Law Reform Act (1982), discussed in chapter 2, provides the legal framework within which the processes of economic readjustment, restructuring of the parent–child relationship, social readjustment, and emotional adjustment occur unless divorce is sought more quickly on the grounds of fault.

Only 25 percent of the Custody Project families were seen following the legal divorce. These families tended to subdivide into two groups: those who had been continuously conflicted from the time of separation (more than three years) and those who, through a change in circumstances of the parents or children, were seeking to alter a decision made previously about the custody and/or access arrangements for their children.

All families referred to the Custody Project had made a decision to separate and had sought legal assistance to implement that decision. Some, while physically together in the matrimonial home, were struggling with economic, social, and emotional adjustment to emotional separation; others, like the Grants, were physically separated. Clinical intervention by the authors therefore was at all points of the separation and divorce process.

Inevitably intervention required an understanding of family systems theory, particularly for the family in crisis. Chapter 7 presents a discussion of the application of that theory to intervention techniques for separating and divorcing families.

The Custody Project families were referred either by the courts or by the parents' lawyers. The parents had already sought the assistance of the judicial-legal system. Custody Project members needed to become familiar with the interface between the legal and the mental health systems. Although the authors had considerable experience in providing clinical services to young people referred by judges of the juvenile court, the rehabilitative focus of that court resulted in a less adversarial process than that found in matrimonial or family litigation. Our legal colleagues, trained to represent a particular family member, found the authors' total family orientation unfamiliar. It is appropriate that we have included in this book an esteemed legal colleague as guest author. A major premise of the Custody Project members is the requirement for productive cooperation between lawyers and clinicians.

Readers will find a number of pervasive themes in the ensuing chapters. The most insistent is the need for collegial consultation and support if clinical intervention is to be objective and effective. In our view, no other area of practice so tests the clinician's personal value system with regard to the family as a social institution, with its roles of husband, and wife, mother and father and children. The concept of 'no-fault' divorce may, in hindsight, have been easier to abandon in law than in the clinician–client relationship. Asssisting families at the point of separation or divorce, even those less bitterly enmeshed than the Gerrards, is not easy.

The chapters dealing with clinical issues in custody and access disputes and intervention techniques reflect another theme. It is our view that both parents hold equal responsibility to ensure the optimal conditions for the continued productive growth of their children. The parental right to an ongoing meaningful relationship with children after family breakdown is not an inherent right but a parental responsibility dependent for its continuation on the degree to which the parent–child interaction contributes to the child positively. The right to access is the child's.

The publication in 1973 of *Beyond the Best Interests of the Child* (Goldstein, Freud, and Solnit) redefined decision making in family breakdown in terms of the primacy of the needs of the child. Appearing as the children's rights movement accelerated, this work engendered great controversy with regard to the custodial parent's right to determine visits between the child and absent parent. The awareness of the public, including the judiciary and lawyers and clinicians, was sharply raised to the needs of the child in a separating or divorcing family. While concurring with the authors' stance that custody and access determination should place the child's need foremost, we differ with their views on the importance of continued access. These will be discussed in chapter 9.

Initially referrals to the Custody Project were for assessment. The resulting clinical opinion was then given verbally to the family and in writing to the referral source, whether lawyers or the court. Referrals were accepted only when the assessor had access to all parties involved in the custody and/or access dispute. Assessment information and observations resulted in case formulation. An opinion by the clinician became a basis for negotiation between counsel and their clients or was scrutinized in court through the process of cross-examination. Acceptance, rejection, or adaptation of the opinion was then reflected in a separation agreement and/or a court order.

Many lawyers have requested assessment of their parent–client alone or with the children whose custody is in dispute. Presumably the lawyer for the other parent is requesting a similar assessment so that each litigant can have his or her expert witness attesting to the quality of parenting capability and parent–child relationship. This "his–her" model is inherently divisive of the family and inadequate in that the assessor has only partial data available. Assessment in a custody and access dispute must focus first on the children's needs and then on the parents' abilities to meet those needs. A one-parent or one-parent-and-child assessment disallows the gathering of information about all the options for the child's future. The parents' interrelationship is central in considering any plan that would allow the child to maintain a significant relationship with both parents. Evaluation of the parental relationship requires that both parents be included in the assessment.

During the past decade, a variety of approaches for intervention with separating and divorcing families have been reported in the literature. Throughout the field of family law, concepts such as conciliation, mediation, and arbitration have been borrowed from the labor relations field as means of family dispute resolution.

The work of the Los Angeles conciliation courts, begun in 1954, became a model for similar projects throughout North America. In Canada, the provincial family courts had a long tradition of court-related support services. Not surprisingly, these courts became the court level in which conciliation services were first attempted.

Divorce mediation as described by Coogler (1978) proposed another means of intervention as an alternative to the adversarial process for separating and divorcing families. Both conciliation and mediation focus on dispute resolution through the assistance of a neutral third party. Coogler distinguishes conciliation from mediation by the extent to which the conciliator or mediator takes responsibility with the disputing parents for examining the issues in dispute and developing options for their resolution. The conciliator offers options, pointing out their advantages and disadvantages; the mediator avoids taking such responsibility so that the family members themselves take the responsibility for the decisions reached. Mediation is more likely to involve the children in the interview sequence, although in both, this is likely to occur at a latter stage or phase.

In describing a twelve-step mediation process, Haynes (1982) describes mediation as a fluid process, with the chronology of the process changing to meet the specific needs of a family. At the eighth step, the author states, "The assessment of the family structure which the mediator has been making at each step of the process is applied at this point to assist the clients in self-determination" (p. 14). Haynes recommends involving the children in the mediation process at the tenth step; Coogler proposes a ten-hour mediation process in which the children are involved at the ninth hour but only in situations in which mediation of the custody and/or access dispute cannot be successful with the parents alone at an earlier stage.

The Custody Project members view conciliation and mediation as very similar processes. Coogler's differentiation of the two by the degree of responsibility taken by the conciliator or mediator in contrast with the clients' for suggesting options for resolving disputes or the advantages and disadvantages of various options appears to be a difference based more in the needs and capabilities of the clients than a substantive difference in intervention technique. This aspect of conciliation or mediation as a differentiating characteristic appears to be analogous to the skilled clinician's selection of the treatment of choice with any client. Not everyone is a candidate for insight-oriented psychotherapy, nor is every client best served by behavior modification.

In the resolution of conflict with regard to the custody and access arrangements for children, conciliators, mediators, and assessors have agreed that the guiding principle must be the least detrimental alternative for the children. To attain this, the parents' commitment to placing their children's needs equal to or above their own is mandatory. The direct involvement of the children in the intervention process promotes this shift in parental stance by the explicit awareness of the children's views and feelings and the clinician's modeling of the importance of the children's position in the dispute.

A further concern is that parents, preoccupied with their own distress, may reach an agreed-upon plan for their children that discounts the children's wishes entirely or precludes consideration of the children's needs. Prior to their contact with the Custody Project, there was considerable discussion with the Gerrards with regard to a custody plan in which the children would have been divided between the parents; the children's own wish to remain together would have been contravened without discussion with them. Their need for mutual support would have been abrogated. The Custody Project members suggest that postponement of the children's involvement in the process of intervention undermines the children's right to be heard and neglects an important means by which the parents' attention to their children's needs can be fostered.

Conciliation and mediation are similar as well in that both generally have been defined as a closed process of intervention in contrast to the open process of assessment. The conciliator-mediator agrees with each parent that any communication will be confidential to the clients and the interviewer, not available to counsel or to any subsequent court proceeding. This closed characteristic is similar to the privileged communication between lawyers and their clients, traditionally protected in law far more stringently than the communication between clients and mental health professionals. One argument on behalf of a closed process has been that parents will be more open and relaxed in providing information to the conciliator-mediator if they feel assured of complete confidentiality. The presumption appears to be that each parent will reveal more about herself or himself than in an open process. It has been our experience, however, that parents disputing custody and/or access initially want to ensure that the clinician knows every possible allegation he or she can make about the other parent. In a family referred by the courts or by counsel, such allegations have usually been previously documented in graphic terms in affidavits.

Polarization has developed among conciliators, mediators, and assessors with regard to the best (presumably most effective) process of intervention. Data have rarely been available to support the protagonists' positions.

The Grants, on the basis of their long, conflicted relationship, Mr. Grant's abduction of Bobby, and Mrs. Grant's application for a court order to deny access between father and son, might have been viewed as a family in which the parents could not communicate sufficiently to work out for their child an agreed plan or mediated solution. Referral for evaluation might have presumed that decision making could be accomplished only by an external resource: a clinical opinion and/or a court order. Alternatively, the Grants might have been referred to a closed mediation process. If an agreement could not have been mediated, however, the family conflict would have had to be referred back to court or for open assessment from which information and a clinical opinion could be derived and made available to counsel or the court. The Grants would then be involved in a two-stage process of intervention. We concur with the concern expressed by Goldstein, Freud, and Solnit (1973) and Benedek and Benedek (1972) that determination of custody and access disputes should reflect a child's sense of time, not that of the parenting adults, clinicians, or the legal-judicial system. A two-step process from closed mediation to open assessment compounds the time of uncertainty for the child and parents.

In the Custody Project members' opinion, mediation relies on the mediator's skill in brief assessment, not unlike crisis intervention. The effective assessment is one in which the children's and parents' needs and strengths are clearly determined with the parents. Both approaches presume an educative component and a firm expectation that parents will resume responsible and rational planning for their children. Briefly, the skilled mediator assesses; the skilled assessor mediates. The more effective process is defined by the needs and capabilities of the family, many families requiring both. To decide the intervention approach before the clinician has contact with all the family members would be an abdication of professional responsibility.

The more salient issue lies in the mediator-assessor's stance in undertaking an open or closed process. In the latter, the clinician by contract is protected from providing expert testimony; the open process of mediation-assessment presumes that the clinician is prepared to provide expert testimony if required. This will be discussed further by Kreindler in chapter 3.

Arbitration, like *conciliation* and *mediation,* is a term borrowed from the labor relations field. Coogler (1978) and Solow and Adams (1977) propose arbitration as a process to be used when mediation cannot resolve the parental dispute. Coogler defines arbitration as an adversarial process in which the disputing parties, with or without counsel, are competing with one another to obtain the arbitrator's favorable decision. Further, the parties by agreement are bound to accept the arbitrator's decision, from which there is no appeal. Solow and Adams report the assessment findings to the court, and an order ensues. In effect, the arbitrator's decision replaces a judicial decision.

The Custody Project members have been unwilling to undertake arbitration. The arguments for this use of mental health professionals with families disputing custody and access—that nonjudicial arbitration is faster, less emotionally damaging to the family members, and less financially costly—do not outweigh the right of families to access to the courts and the obligation of the state through the courts to adjudicate what constitutes the child's best interest.

In summary, the Custody Project members recommend that intervention with families disputing custody and access include all family members and significant others in an open process in which a clear expectation is made that the parents utilizing the assessment information about themselves and their children will develop a postseparation plan themselves. Only if every effort to facilitate this fails is an imposed plan based in a clinical opinion necessary.

Concurrent with the controversy over kinds of intervention, debate has raged equally hotly over the best custody planning. Sole custody, the traditional plan, although supported firmly by Goldstein, Freud, and Solnit (1973), was in disrepute in many quarters, viewed as a denial of the rights of the absent parent and inherently detrimental to both the rights and needs of the children. Joint custody was vehemently proposed by many authors, again rarely with data to support their position. To this controversy, the longitudinal study of Wallerstein and Kelly (1980) brought invaluable information in documenting the responses of children at different stages of development to the decisions made with regard to their custody and access or visitation with the absent parent. Joint custody as an arrangement in law giving parents equal guardianship and decision-making power in child rearing began to be reviewed as an alternative with variations possible in allowing for coparenting or shared parenting, the children in the care and control of either parent according to the child's needs and the abilities and circumstances of the parents.

Less attention has been given to access arrangements. There is much to suggest that access disputes are more difficult and more protracted than custody disputes, thereby extending the postseparation conflict, with ensuing damage for all family members, particularly the visited or visiting child.

Our experience and research findings indicate that separating and divorcing families are no more a homogenous group than are young offenders or families of schizophrenics. Each of these subpopulations in spite of similarities requires varying kinds of intervention determined by their differences. Similarly, families unable independently to resolve their conflict regarding custody and access of children appear to require a range or continuum of techniques of intervention, not mutually exclusive but integrated by the skillful clinician and a range of planning alternatives that provides for the least detrimental alternative for the children.

In preparing this book, we hope that our experience and research findings will be of assistance to others working with families caught in family breakdown.

2

Historical Perspective of Custody and Access Disputes: A Lawyer's View

James C. MacDonald

C ustody in the broad sense connotes the whole bundle of rights and powers vested in a parent over a child. It includes the right to make decisions for the child relating to such matters as medical treatment, education, and religious training, on the one hand, and the right to have the day-to-day care and control of the child, on the other. Sometimes, especially in the nonlegal literature, the two aspects of custody are separated, giving two meanings to the word. One aspect is called legal custody (the right to make decisions) and the other physical custody (the right to daily care). In this chapter, the word will be used in its broad sense to include both legal and physical custody.

Unless the child suffers from a physical or mental disability, custody does not last indefinitely. It comes to an end when the child attains its majority (eighteen years of age in many jurisdictions) or marries. Usually before that time the rights to decision making and care have eroded somewhat as the child develops a mind of his or her own. As Lord Denning stated in a 1969 English case, "Custody is a dwindling right. . . . It starts with a right of control and ends with little more than advice" (Hewer v. Bryant (1969), 3 All E.R. 518 at 582). Custody is almost always awarded subject to the right of the other parent to spend time with the child. This right is referred to in England and Canada as access and in the United States as visitation.

In most states and provinces in these countries, the law of custody is derived from the law of England and speaks of the best interests of the child. The content of this notion of best interests and its application has a fascinating history from which certain themes can be extracted, among them the following:

1. Presumptive parental superiority.
2. Conduct of the parents.
3. Emotional tie to the child.
4. Dispute resolution.

Paternal Presumption

In the early days of the English law, the father was considered the parent naturally endowed to have custody of the children. This preeminence was accepted without question in any dispute against the mother. In those rare instances where, despite the social and economic pressures of the time, a separation did occur, the mother had absolutely no rights to the custody of the children, and she faced the real prospect of never seeing them again.

Sir William Blackstone, an English jurist who lived from 1723 to 1780, described the law of the day when he wrote that "a mother, as such, is entitled to no power, but only to reverence and respect" (Blackstone, Commentaries, 19th London ed. 1857, p. 373).

The father's right persisted even where the children were very young. An example often cited is the case of *R. v. De Manneville* (1804, 102 Eng. Rep. 1054) where the father was awarded custody of the child notwithstanding the fact that it was an eight-month-old infant still "feeding at the breast" and the further fact that marriage breakdown was caused by the father's cruelty. The mother did not even have ameliorating right of access or visitation. In the case of *Ball v. Ball* (1827, 2 Sim. 35), the vice-chancellor refused not only the mother's petition for custody but also her alternative claim for access because of a lack of jurisdiction or power to grant this relief.

There were occasions when the courts refused to enforce the father's right to custody because contact with him would result in extreme moral or physical danger to the child, but it was not until 1839 in Talfourd's Act (2 & 3 Vict. c.90) that the court had jurisdiction to make an award in the mother's favor. By this legislation, the court, in an appropriate case, was empowered to give the mother custody but only until the child reached the age of seven years. It is important to note that if the mother did obtain custody of her baby, the statute comtemplated that custody would revert to the father before or at the age of seven. His presumed parental superiority was still strongly embedded in the law. Talfourd's Act merely recognized that he was not equipped to breast feed and, according to the social mores of the time, could not be expected to wipe running noses. Subject to these concessions, there was little doubt that the father was the preferred single parent. In 1883, the Court of Appeal of England stated with reference to the father's right of custody in the case of *Re Agar-Ellis* (24 Chanc. L.R. 317, 339), "This Court holds the principle that . . . it is for the general interest of families, and for the general interest of children, and really for the interest of the particular infant, that the court should not, except in very extreme cases interfere with the discretion of the father, but leave to him the responsibility of exercising that power (over the child) which nature has given him."

In exceptional circumstances involving a danger to the child, the courts would intervene in favor of the mother, first by merely refusing to enforce the father's absolute right so that she took charge of the child for lack of a legal custodian. Later, as the courts acquired jurisdiction to do so, positive orders naming the mother as the custodial parent were made. Talfourd's Act began the process of bestowing jurisdiction, a first cautious step limiting the mother's custody right to the age of seven for the child. Not until 1873 was the age of the child extended to sixteen years, and in 1886 it was extended to the age of twenty-one.

By the late nineteenth century, the courts had jurisdiction to award custody of the child to either the father or the mother, but in the exercise of that jurisdiction the claim of the father was superior. The onus was on the mother to show that harm would befall the child if kept in the father's custody; if she could not, then she was left empty-handed.

As we entered the twentieth century, the presumed paternal superiority came under attack. The courts in England began the development in the *case* law, which by 1925 became part of the *statute* law in a provision declaring that neither the father nor the mother would be regarded as having a custody claim superior to the other. The same legislation restated the principle that in deciding questions of custody, the court should give the welfare of the child first and paramount consideration.

The father's presumed superiority was abolished by case and statute law, which declared that the father and the mother had equal rights to the custody of their children; however, further developments in the case law took the mother beyond her rise to equal status. The nature and sharpness of the transition is stated by Roman and Haddad (1978, p. 23):

> With a tidiness that is as surprising as it is rare, the 1920's can be pinpointed as the moment when history's long alliance with the rights of the father ended. From the 1920's on, mothers were virtually assured of the custody of their children even though the mother's paramount claims are not now, nor were they at any time based on the law.

The origins of the change can be traced in part to the trend to urbanization and industrialization, which forced fathers to work away from home and to leave child rearing to mothers, and the development of the science of psychology, which suddenly discovered the maternal instinct, or the concept that good mothering produces emotionally healthy children. Weitzman and Dixon (1979, p. 481) state:

> The wisdom of the maternal presumption was also supported by psychologists and child development specialists who emphasized the unique relationship between an infant and its mother. These professionals asserted that "young children needed a mother in order to develop optimally" and that women were uniquely suited, biologically and psychologically for the task of rearing children. The social science dogma was that men and women were

biologically destined to play not only different but mutually exclusive roles as parents; that an inherent nurturing ability disposes women to be more interested in and more able to care for children than are men; and that for their well-being, children needed mothers in a way that they do not need fathers.

In brief, by the late 1930s it was considered unnatural for a father to want or to have the sole care of his children.

Although directed to make custody awards on the basis of the best interests of the child, the courts typically held this to mean that the child should not be separated from the mother. This evolved into a judicial presumption that other things being equal, the love and nurturance of a mother was always in the child's and the community's best interest.

Motherhood became revered by the judges. Some of the finest eulogies to mothers were given in the courts of law. We find these passages:

> For a boy of such tender years nothing can be an adequate substitute for mother love—for that constant ministration required during the period of nurture that only a mother can give because in her alone is duty swallowed up in desire; in her alone is service expressed in terms of love. She alone has the patience and sympathy required to mold and soothe the infant mind in its adjustment to its environment. The difference between fatherhood and motherhood in this respect is fundamental. (Jenkins v. Jenkins, 1921, 173 Wis. 592)

> There is but a twilight zone between a mother's love and the atmosphere of heaven (Tuter v. Tuter, 1938, 120 S.W.2d 203, 205 Ct. App.)

> Mother love is a dominant trait in even the weakest of women, and as a general thing, surpasses the paternal affection for the common offspring, and moreover, a child needs a mother's care even more than a father's. For these reasons, the courts are loath to deprive the mother of the custody of her children. (Miller 1979, p. 41)

> It is not for a Court to rend the most sacred ties of nature which bind a mother to her children, except in extreme cases. (Miller 1979, p. 43)

Today mental health professionals are telling us that early studies in maternal deprivation failed to apply the same tests to father. When attention is now turned to father loss, it is perhaps not surprising that the father is also found to be an important figure to the child. The degree of comparative importance is something that cannot be measured and if it could would not really matter.

There is a burgeoning belief, still mostly at the grass-roots level, that parenting is a shared responsibility that must be made to continue after parental separation. Witness, for instance, the popular movement for joint custody. Many professionals, clinicians, lawyers, courts, and possibly significant groups in the community have not quite accepted this premise. Mothers are still on a pedestal and in the absence of unusual circumstances are not likely to lose custody, if contested. Parenting, taking opinions across the board in our society, is still thought of as mothering. In the movie *Kramer v. Kramer,* we know the court should have given custody of the boy to his father and was wrong in not doing so. Why? Because he was the better "mother." The boy's mother was not there; she had abdicated and saw the child only twice in eighteen months. The mothering was done by the father. The boy's perception of his father's mothering was made obvious when the father was late on one occasion and the boy pointed out that "all the *other* mothers were on time." When we in the audience were convinced that the father was a good "mother," he became a believable candidate for custody of the boy.

Does this mean that to succeed on a custody claim, fathers must prove that they are good mothers? In the eyes of most courts, the answer is probably yes. We still believe that the mother has a superior right to custody, contrary to the statute law, which speaks of equal rights. She wins over 90 percent of the time.

Conduct

The history of moral conduct of parents is a further element in family law. Custody is often one of the several claims in a divorce petition, and it is through the eyes of the divorce courts that the part conduct plays in custody determinations can best be seen.

Earlier marriage was governed by the ecclesiastical law as ordained by the church. Woman was Adam's rib, and upon marriage man and woman again became as one flesh. The woman lost her capacity as a legal person. All her property rights were automatically transferred to her husband, along with some of her personal rights. Incompatibility of temperament was never a grievance recognized in English law because it was the duty of the wife to adapt her temperament to that of her husband. There could be no such thing as incompatibility, or if there was, it was her fault.

Marriage was a fusion of opposite sexes for life; there was no such thing as divorce. The purpose of marriage was to have children.

Wealth, in the form of landholdings and the rights and privileges attached to them, was passed through the generations from father to son. It was important economically to the father that the children be his.

Adultery was much more culpable on the part of the wife than on the part of the husband. She was his property, and he was entitled to grade A goods— that is, goods that were unadulterated. If she was unfaithful, he could bring a legal action against her lover for money damages, an action known as criminal conversation. The wife did not have the same right against her husband or her husband's lover. A further reason that is also part of the rationale of the first is that modern methods of contraception were unknown, leaving the worrisome possibility that the wife's adultery might introduce extraneous lines into the inheritance stream. These forces gave rise to the view that adultery is a sin much more easily forgivable in a man than in a woman, and it produced the notorious double standard.

Adultery was a sin, and more than this, it was equated with the spiritual death of the marriage, eventually giving justification to divorce. Divorce through the courts entered England in 1857. The grounds for divorce were essentially adultery, the prime matrimonial offense. Lord Denning, one of England's most eminent jurists, made this comment in 1973:

> When parliament in 1857 introduced divorce by the courts of law, it based it on the doctrine of the matrimonial offence. This affected all that followed. If a person was the guilty party in a divorce suit, it went hard with him or her. It affected so many things. *The custody of the children depended on it.* So did the award of maintenance. To say nothing of the standing in society. So serious were the consequences that divorce suits were contested at great length and at much cost. (Wachtel v. Wachtel, 1973, 1 All E.R. 829, p. 835; italics added)

Lord Denning's statement is correct, of course, but it should be remembered that the consequences were immeasurably harder on the wife if she were the guilty party than if the case were the other way around. Although the principle had been developing that the welfare of the child was paramount in determining questions of custody, the judicial mind was unable to separate the welfare of the child from questions of sexual morality of the parents. If a wife-mother was guilty of adultery, she not only lost the marriage but custody and financial support as well. Her unfaithfulness as a wife completely wiped out her virtues as a mother and blinded the court to what was happening to the children. Her transgression may have been discreet, an isolated occurrence known only to a few and certainly not to the children. She may have been otherwise the perfect parent: loving, warm, sensitive, mentally stimulating, firm when need be but not harsh, and the children's primary source of security and happiness. No matter. As Sir Cresswell Cresswell, one of the early divorce judges, said one hundred years ago in *Seddon v. Seddon,* "It will probably have a salutory effect on the interests of public morality, that it should be known that a woman, if found guilty of adultery, will forfeit, as far as this Court is concerned, all right to the custody of or access to her children" (Seddon v. Seddon, 1962, 164 E.R. 1146).

An adulteress was an outcast. Once branded with the scarlet letter, she could be removed from her children and never see them again. The end of her complete banishment is marked by the case of *Stark v. Stark,* decided by the

English Court of Appeal in 1910. Here the mother had been divorced on the ground of adultery and married the corespondent. Her sixteen-year-old daughter who was in the custody of the father ran away to live with her, the mother. The father brought proceedings for contempt of court against the mother, and she was jailed for a short period. She appealed the contempt conviction, and the Court of Appeal, breaking new ground, said that the adultery "ought not to be regarded for all time and in all circumstances as sufficient to disentitle the mother to access to her daughter, or even to the custody of her daughter" (Stark v. Stark, 1910, P. 190). A single act of adultery could be explained away, and the court was to allow the mother the custody and care of her children, notwithstanding her temporary fall from grace. A continuing extramarital relationship was not so easily overlooked, however.

For many more years, such a public flaunting of adultery was condemned, and the parent involved—again, more especially the mother—was deprived of custody. This was now happening because the living arrangement, so the courts said, was a bad moral example for the children. Whether or not we think the cure was worse than the disease, we can at least give our approval to the focus on the children and the concern for their welfare. This is certainly better than having the courts grant or withhold custody as an example to others who might be contemplating separation or to punish.

Attitudes toward informal living arrangements change as statistics for marriage breakdown soar and the number of persons cohabiting without marriage increases. Less emphasis is placed on the form of the relationship and more on whether the home environment meets the needs of the child for stability and affection. This is illustrated in the Ontario case of *Hill v. Hill* (1975). The trial judge had deprived the mother of the children because she was living with her male friend. When the case came before the court of appeal, custody of the children was restored to the mother, with the court ignoring the moral implications of the situation and stressing the realities of the relationship between the children and the adult male in the new household. "There was no evidence," the court of appeal said, "that [the man's] conduct towards the children was any different from that which might be exhibited by a responsible and loving step-father" (Hill v. Hill, 1975, 6 O.R.2d, 474).

Despite the fact that conduct has decreased in importance, it can still be invoked in many instances to the prejudice of a custody case. In 1962, Lord Denning stated,

> Whilst no doubt the mother is a good mother in one sense of the word, in that she looks after the children well, giving them love and, as far as she can, security, one must remember that to be a good mother involves not only looking after the children, but making and keeping a home for them with their father, bringing up the two children in the love and security of the home

with both parents. Insofar as she herself by her conduct broke up that home, she is not a good mother. (Re L., 1962, 3 All E.R. 1, at 3)

A judge of the Supreme Court in Ontario quoted this passage with approval in 1971 (Neilsen v. Neilsen, 1971, 16 D.L.R.3d, 33), and there are other scattered examples of where evidence of initiating the separation is taken as evidence of an incapacity to parent. A note of welcome relief, however, was sounded by the Supreme Court of Canada in 1976 when it made the distinction that a woman who is "well-nigh impossible" as a wife may nevertheless be a satisfactory mother (Talsky v. Talsky, 1976, R.F.L. 26).

In terms of community attitudes, homosexuality is probably today's version of the nineteenth century adultery, but there are signs that it too is being separated from the issue of parenting. A judgment of a case giving serious treatment to the issue was first made in 1975 by the Saskatchewan supreme court trial bench. The judge commented:

> Since the commencement of this trial, I have been much concerned about the weight which I could give on the issue of custody to the undoubted fact that the mother leads a homosexual existence and probably will continue to do so. I know of no judicial pronouncements on that point. It seems to me that homosexuality on the part of the parent is a fact to be considered along with all of the other evidence in the case. It should not be considered a bar in itself to a parent's right to custody (Case v. Case, 1974, 18 R.F.L. 132, at 136).

In deciding against the mother and granting custody to the father, the judge excused the fact of homosexuality but not the way she championed the cause and the way she failed to provide a stable routine in the household.

A second case involving homosexuality was decided in Alberta in the next year, 1976, where custody was granted to the homosexual mother. Part of the explanation lies in the fact that, sexual orientation apart, the mother on the evidence was a more suitable person to have the care of the children than was her drug-abusing husband. Nevertheless, we must be impressed by the fact that the court went beyond looking at homosexuality versus drugs to other facts bearing on the needs of the children. The court said:

> One must guard against magnifying the issue of homosexuality as it applies to the capacity for performing the duties of a parent. Heterosexuals produce children who become homosexual and the evidence of the psychiatrist and phychologist in this case did not indicate that the odds of becoming or being a homosexual would increase solely by reason of being reared by a homosexual parent. Mrs. K. is a good mother, capable of caring for the physical and emotional needs of her child. She would be physically present on a continuous basis. . . . I am satisfied that . . . [her] relationship will be discreet and will not be flaunted to the children or to the community at large.

The judge then dealt with possible social prejudice realistically:

> I considered the potential effect on the child of negative reaction emanating
> from the other children at school and from the community should the exact
> relationship . . . become well known. . . . A heterosexual living with a part-
> ner of the opposite sex but of a different race would be equally likely to suffer
> from negative community reaction and this in turn would be visited upon the
> children. (K. v. K., 1975, 23 R.F.L. 58, at 64)

Emotional Ties

The third theme influencing the determination of custody and access disputes
embraces parent–child psychological attachments. This subject has a much
more recent legal history. In *Re Thain,* a case in 1926 in England, Mr. Justice
Eve stated:

> It is said that the little girl will be greatly distressed and upset at parting from
> Mr. and Mrs. Jones. I can quite understand that it may be so, but at her
> tender age, one knows from experience how mercifully transient are the
> effects of partings and other sorrows, and how soon the novelty of fresh sur-
> roundings and new associations effaces the recollection of former days with
> kind friends, and I cannot attach much weight to this aspect of the case. (Re
> Thain, 1926, Ch. 676, at 684)

There can be no doubt that the sentiment expressed in this quotation was the
conventional judicial wisdom of the day. Grief at parting is transient, was the
belief, and was therefore a circumstance deserving of little weight.

By 1965 this view was repudiated, and we hear Mr. Justice Cross:

> But the child psychiatrists who give evidence in these cases nowadays,
> though they do not always agree in detail, all emphasize the risks involved in
> transferring young children from the care of one person to another, partic-
> ularly between the age of one-and-a-half and three, while as to the view of
> [Mr. Justice] Eve, . . . , Dr. S., when they put it to him plainly regarded them
> much as Thomas Huxley would have regarded the suggestion that the world
> came into being in the manner set out in the first chapter of Genesis. (Re W.,
> 1965, 3 All E.R. 231, at 248)

In Ontario, the danger of uprooting the child from familiar surroundings
and established relationships was recognized in the case of *Re Moores and
Feldstein* (1973, 12 R.F.L. 273), where the foster parents succeeded on
appeal in keeping a four-year-old daughter against the claim of her biological
mother who had not seen her since shortly after birth. The blood tie was not

sufficient to overcome the fact that the mother was now a stranger. After this breakthrough, the principle was established in 1984 for all of the courts in Canada by the country's Supreme Court in *King v. Low* (Supreme Court of Canada, Dickson, C.J., Ritchie, Beetz, McIntyre, Chouinard, Lamr, and Wilson, J.J., March, 14, 1985). In this case, the court held that the bonding between the child and the adoptive parents was of prime importance in determining that it was in the best interests of the child to remain with the adoptive parents over the objections of the natural mother who had changed her mind and wanted the child returned to her. This kind of bonding had earlier achieved popular recognition in the book *Beyond the Best Interests of the Child* (Goldstein, Freud, and Solnit 1973), with its explanation of psychological parenting.

From a historical point of view, the significance of giving consideration in law to the emotional tie is that it gives status to the child. To consider his or her feelings is to consider the child as a person; conversely, not to consider the child's feelings is to consider him or her as a chattel, which is exactly what we have done for so long. Having almost equal significance is the fact that the focus on parent–child attachment is becoming a primary concern. In theory at least, this implies that in custody and access disputes, the child is considered first and the parents second.

This discussion on the presumption in favor of the father, then of the mother, and the place given to conduct in custody cases is intended to show how little attention has been paid in history to the individual needs of the child. Cases decided on the basis of preconceived notions of parental superiority or on the basis of so-called right and wrong conduct address the needs of the child only by accident. The trend continues as we are reminded by Mr. Justice Bayda dissenting in the case of *Wakaluk* decided in 1977 by the Saskatchewan Court of Appeal:

> No one bothered to bring forward much information in respect of the two individuals who of all the persons likely to be affected by these proceedings least deserve to be ignored—the children. . . . No evidence was led to establish the intellectual, moral, emotional and physical needs of each child. Apart from the speculation that these children are "ordinary" (whatever that means) there is nothing on which to base a reasoned particular best interests in his own particular situation. We do not act in the best interests of the children, as a class, we act in the best interests of this particular child. (Wakaluk v. Wakaluk, 1976, 25 R.F.L. 292, at 299)

We improve the quality of data by the direct marshaling of facts through separate representation of the child and encourage family assessments by child specialists. We avoid presumptions and preconceived ideas about what is good for the child and rely on what one article refers to as "meticulous fact finding" in individual cases (Foster and Freed 1978).

In any individual case, what might the best interest of the child amount to? John Coons and Robert Mnookin (1978, p. 395) state:

> Deciding what is best for a child poses a question no less ultimate than the purposes and values of life itself. Should the judge be primarily concerned with the child's happiness; or with the child's spiritual and religious training? Should the judge be concerned with the economic "productivity" of the child when he grows up? Are the primary values of life in warm, interpersonal relationships, or in discipline and self-sacrifice? Are stability and security for a child more desirable than intellectual stimulation? These questions could be elaborated endlessly. And yet, where is the judge to look for the set of values that should inform the choice of what is best for the child? Normally, the custody statutes do not themselves give content or relative weight to the pertinent values. If one looks to society at large, one finds neither a clear consensus as to the best child rearing strategies nor an appropriate hierarchy of ultimate values. There are only private views. In an exceptionally diverse society that is deeply marked by racial and religious divisions, highly varied in economy, geography, and even in the degree of urbanization, there is no consensus about the good life for children.

At this point lawyers throw up their hands and say with resignation that we are not looking to the best interests in any ideal sense and agree with Goldstein, Freud, and Solnit that we are content with the least detrimental alternative. We are content to choose the custody placement that causes the least harm to the child.

Dispute Resolution

There are further complexities. To address some of them, we should look for a moment at the system used to select the custody placement when parents disagree: the adversary system.

The adversary system works best when the question of fact to be determined can be isolated as a single point decisive of all the rights involved. For instance, in an action for damages arising out of a car accident, was the defendant driver keeping a proper lookout in the split second before the collision? In a criminal case on a charge of murder, do the accused's fingerprints match those found on the weapon? In an estate matter, were the witnesses present when the testator signed the will? The system might also be able to find, as one jurist claimed, such unobservable facts as the state of a person's digestion.

These are pointed, simple, straightforward questions frozen in the past where the facts do not change. But with more complex questions that are partly future oriented, the system does not work so well. It is extremely difficult to find as a fact whether the child would be more or less secure in a new setting and more difficult still to find as a fact how he or she will feel in two years. Some would say that these questions are so difficult for the system that it makes no sense to ask them and expect sensible answers.

Another feature of how the system deals with questions is that it usually offers only either-or choices. Who should have custody: this parent or that parent? Who is better: the mother or the father? In most cases as far as the good of the child is concerned, this is probably the wrong kind of question altogether. A better kind might be, How can the mother and father collaborate after the separation to continue the coparenting of their children? But this kind of question is beyond the capacity of the court. No one is accusing anyone of anything, and there is nothing for the judge to referee.

In the past, the system worked well because the questions were appropriate. Did the respondent commit adultery on the night of January 14–15? Did she desert her husband? Does he take drugs? If these are the questions we still want answered and no others, the system will continue to work. But in most cases, the questions are much more complicated and more often than not tend to overload the decision-making system.

There is another defect, which is more difficult to conceptualize. The system lawyers use to find the best or least detrimental alternative relies on building up credits for the client and pointing to debits for the opponent. Experience shows that this process unleashes anger and hostile forces that sometimes destroy the best alternative. We have this dilemma. The very attempt to determine the best alternative generates forces that put it out of reach. It is like trying to see a particle that is smaller than a beam of light. Physicists say that we cannot see without light striking the object and reflecting back to the eye. If the particle is so small and weightless that the light pushes it away without meeting enough resistance to be bounced back, the particle will never come into view. In some cases, is the goal of the best interests of the child unattainable because the adversary process keeps pushing it away?

In summary, we have the following possibilities of failure. First, the question of best interests is impossible for the courts to answer because there are no generally accepted standards. There are only individual values that lead to a disparity of treatment. Two cases, each having similar facts and each proceeding before a different judge, should receive similar treatment. If they do not and the cases are decided differently because the judges have different value systems, the system operates by the luck of the draw, which is offensive to our sense of justice. The second possibility of failure is that the question of the child's best interests is too complicated for the adversary system to address and answer sensibly. And the third possibility is that in attempting to answer the question, the process itself may destroy the alternative it should be attempting to preserve and implement.

Confronted with these possibilities of failure, short of refusing to become involved in a custody case, what should a lawyer do? For most cases, he or she must find and use a different system. Fortunately, a different and vastly improved system is emerging from a better understanding among lawyers of the needs of children and from an insight into the principles and methods used by mental health professionals.

The lawyer begins to see himself or herself with two clients, the parent and the child. It cannot be helped, because all too soon he or she will hear the voice of the mental health professional saying, "What I would like to know is, when is somebody going to start thinking about the child?" Startled, the lawyer asks, "What do you mean?" . . . and there it starts. Soon the lawyer is on the telephone adopting a persuasive manner first with the parent client and then with the other lawyer, convincing them that there ought to be an assessment involving the whole family and that it should be flexible enough to swing into mediation with a view to settlement of the custody issue.

A referral is made to the assessment-mediation process. The lawyer cooperates with this process by working on the sidelines and participating more actively when needed but concentrating on the shared goal of achieving the best solution for the family with the least amount of pain.

Conclusion

What is our direction in the future? I think we are heading to a graduated process for the resolution of custody questions. First, parties and their lawyers will be encouraged to settle the question themselves in a problem-solving, nonadversarial atmosphere focusing on the needs of the child in an attempt to devise a custody and access plan that will maximize the satisfaction of these needs. Second, if the parties and their lawyers cannot settle the question, the matter proceeds to mediation. This part introduces a qualified child specialist who will assist in the settlement process, contributing expertise to help develop the options or alternatives and remove obstacles blocking agreement.

The process in these two steps must be given every possible assistance needed to achieve their goals, including persuasive direction and admonition from the court. The courts should not remain aloof and say merely that if the parents cannot agree between themselves, it stands ready to make the decision. The courts must show that they are united with the rest of the community in believing that decisions made by the family, with the help of a child behavior specialist where necessary, are generally better than those that the court imposed. Most people want to respect the law and will be persuaded by what they perceive the courts wish them to do. If the judge speaking from a position of authority were to give the appropriate leadership, many more couples would be genuinely motivated to seek consensual solutions focusing on what is best for the child.

Judicial leadership may not be wanting for long. It has expressed itself in the approach of the conciliation courts having jurisdiction in many parts of the United States. Awareness is a necessary preliminary condition to solving any problem. In Canada, judges are coming to realize that in a world of subjective values and human imperfection, only the family knows what is best for the child and only with the cooperation of all family members is it likely to be achieved. Individualized justice, a much-desired goal, is more possible through a conferencing rather than an adversarial approach.

There will still be some cases that cannot be resolved by any legitimate means other than through litigation. The court must be available for these cases; no one doubts that. But they must be used only as a place of last resort, or, to put the matter in a way said to me by a child psychiatrist and that is not as contradictory as it sounds, "The courts should be there, but they should not be used."

Current legislation in many jurisdictions gives recognition to the value of assessment and mediation. It is but a short step to the implementation of mediation as a precondition to litigation. Finally, however, it will be the mental health professional and the lawyer working together who will make the process work.

Note

The publisher and author wish to thank the Carswell Company Limited for their kind permission to reproduce material from "Toward a Theory of Children's Rights" by J.E. Coons and R.H. Mnookin, which appeared in *The Child and the Courts,* edited by I.F.G. Baxter and M.A. Eberts, and published by The Carswell Company Limited in 1978.

3

The Role of the Mental Health Professions in Custody and Access Disputes

Simon Kreindler

The history of the involvement of mental health professionals with families at the point of family breakdown is short when compared with the involvement of lawyers and the courts. Indeed, psychiatry, social work, and psychology were in their infancy until the turn of the century, their development to be shaped by their differing roots and vast societal changes.

Professional Evolution of Mental Health Professions

Psychiatry, a medical specialty, was not far beyond the era in which mental illness was thought to be caused by evil spirits. During the second half of the nineteenth century, the recognition of the etiological importance of physiological factors in mental illness resulted in the development of more humane approaches to treatment.

Social work in the nineteenth century focused on social reforms and services to specific disadvantaged subgroups: the illegitimate and the destitute.

Psychology, from its base in philosophy and biology, has been described as "that branch of science which deals with the mind and mental processes, especially in relation to human and animal behaviour" (Dorland's Illustrated Medical Dictionary, 1974).

In 1895 Freud first outlined his theories of personality in a work written with Joseph Breuer. The influence of psychoanalytic theory on psychiatry, social work, and psychology was immeasurable, giving a new emphasis to historical and developmental factors as causes of psychological problems in the individual. The evolution and application of psychoanalytic theory became processes in which the three disciplines met. The establishment in 1909 of the National Committee for Mental Hygiene became an arena in which interdisciplinary acquaintanceship occurred. Psychiatry moved into the community, social work developed the psychosocial approach to individuals, and psychology brought methods of individual assessment as its contribution to the multidisciplinary team.

During the first quarter of this century, an ever-expanding body of theoretical knowledge and the development of techniques of individual treatment occurred against a backdrop of rapid societal change. As North America moved from being primarily a rural, agricultural society to one with an industrial base with large urban populations, a number of simultaneous important changes occurred. Women began to work, to earn money, and to own property. Their increased self-sufficiency has made it possible for them to support children in their custody, their bargaining power playing an important part in altering the long-established bias favoring fathers as the parental custodian of choice.

The public education movement and improved child labor and child protection laws reflected society's increased interest in children. The public's interest in child development, again influenced by Freud's recognition that the roots of much adult psychopathology lay in earlier childhood experiences, set the stage for the child guidance movement. It was hoped that early intervention with troubled children could prevent later mental illness. The rapid proliferation following World War I of child guidance clinics brought active collaboration among psychiatry, social work, and psychology. The traditional model held that the psychiatrist treated the "sick" or disturbed child; the social worker focused on parent reeducation, albeit primarily with the mother alone; and the psychologist tested or measured individual differences among children and among parents.

Whereas the rearing of children had previously been the exclusive responsibility of parents, the child guidance movement fostered the development of professionals who regarded the training of parents in child management as one of their prime mandates.

The success of the child guidance clinics was mixed. As Caplan and Caplan (1967) have pointed out, the clinics did provide the opportunity for study, treatment, and research into a variety of clinical conditions, as well as serving as training facilities for mental health professionals. However, the assumption that a child would be easier to treat than an adult or could be treated more quickly or at a lesser cost failed to be borne out. At the same time, the emphasis given to early case finding resulted in an uncovering of far more cases than could possibly be dealt with given the available resources:

> Instead of the public health focus on the total population, as had been the original dream of the mental hygiene movement, the [child guidance clinics] slipped back into the traditional pattern of dealing exclusively with a relatively small number of individual patients. (Caplan and Caplan 1967, p. 1503)

Although the idealistic fervor of the child guidance movement was eventually somewhat blunted by the realities of dealing with the seemingly limitless population of patients, by emotional disorders that seemed resistant to the best available treatment, and by social conditions that could not be readily changed, the momentum it had developed contributed to the broader endeavor of community mental health that followed it. Mental health professionals became more involved in working cooperatively with educators, the courts, and the police.

In Austria, August Aichorn (1964) pointed out the connection between criminal behavior in the parent and delinquency in the child and was one of the pioneers in applying psychoanalytic principles in his work with delinquent boys. Shortly after the development of the first juvenile courts in North America, clinical services were established at the request of the judiciary. In the paternalistic philosophy of the juvenile courts, mental health professionals were sought to find means of rehabilitating "misguided youth." Through this the mental health professions and the justice system began a process of collaboration qualitatively different from the contact shared in the more formal adversarial context of the criminal justice system. Their collaboration raised the awareness of the justice system to psychoanalytic theory regarding the primary importance of the mother for normal child development. By the mid-1920s, the "tender years" presumption had reversed the earlier presumption of fathers as the preferred custodial parent.

World War II created a manpower crisis in the mental health field, which led in the immediate postwar era to the broader application of group and family therapy approaches. The systems approach to the family as a unit, where the child was viewed as just one component in a complex system that could malfunction at many different levels and for many different reasons, internal and external in origin, represented an important theoretical development.

As the divorce rate began to climb in the mid-1960s, mental health professionals who had developed considerable expertise in working collaboratively with the courts, police, lawyers, educators, and social agencies increasingly were being called upon to advise parents, lawyers, and the judiciary in contested cases of custody and access. To this role, the mental health professionals brought a body of knowledge in human behavior, interviewing skills, and psychotherapy, using it to ameliorate individuals' and families' distress.

The framework for intervention differed within and among the professional disciplines, but the goal of inducing change so that the client's or patient's life could be more productive and satisfying was the same. Treatment theories included insight-oriented psychotherapies, behavioral modification, structural family therapy, cognitive therapy, and environmental manipulation.

In working with separating and divorcing families, the mental health professionals were required to review their definition of *therapeutic*. Previously viewed as assisting marital couples, families, or individuals to restore their intrafamilial relationships to a previous, often idealized, homeostatic state, each clinician was required to reevaluate the appropriateness of his or her position. It was necessary to distinguish between the clinician's legitimate role in alleviating intrapsychic or interpersonal distress from the clients' or patients' right to make their own decisions with regard to separation or divorce.

The temptation to treat the individuals and resolve conflicts from the past needed to be resisted. Clinicians had to accept that if they were to assist family members at the point of separation and disorganization and attempt to assist them to reorganize for the future, then past events could not be changed, but how they could be thought about and evaluated could be altered so that the past would not be brought destructively into the present and future.

Although considerable knowledge had been gained about separating and divorcing families as a population subgroup, less was known about parents' or children's reactions at the point of family breakdown (Goode 1949). Clinicians undertaking to work with separating and divorcing families had to acquire some knowledge of the judicial system, relevant legislation, and the rules for providing expert testimony. Many mental health professionals have experienced difficulty in bridging the gap created by the difference in professional orientation between lawyers and themselves (Westman 1971). Mental health professionals from their background of treatment and family orientation apply a therapeutic model to the separating or divorcing family, tending to ignore the legal rights of individual family members. The lawyer, trained to place the client's interests before all others, may ignore the damaging effect on other family members, thus affecting adversely their ability to reorganize their lives after the legal process is completed. When the clinician becomes particularly invested in one family member, he or she risks advocating for that client with inevitable loss of objectivity in relation to other family members. When the lawyer becomes invested in family members other than the client—for example, the child—he or she risks becoming the family therapist. In either eventuality, professional roles become fuzzy, and confusion rather than productive cooperation results.

As the demand for both legal and clinical services for separating and divorcing families has risen, both professional groups have had to grapple with adaptation of their traditional roles and techniques. In many jurisdictions, legislation has been passed to ensure that the child's interests are paramount. In representing their parent client, lawyers have had to heighten their awareness of this concept in advising their client. They have had to struggle with the parameters of child representation: is their obligation to put forward the child's wishes, the child's needs, or both?

The mental health professions, despite their traditional wariness of courts and lawyers, their traditional aversion to advice giving, and their preference for a more reflective and nondirective stance with clients, have had to become familiar with court processes and relevant legislation. They have had to learn to utilize a more directive, proactive approach with clients. Thus, both lawyers and mental health professionals are in a period of professional change, reassessing their individual roles while daily on a case-by-case basis trying to work effectively with one another. Traveling by different paths, colored by their differing backgrounds, some consensus has nevertheless been reached on some points:

1. Extensive litigation in family disputes is financially and emotionally costly.

2. Children have a major stake in their own future following parental separation and have a right to be heard.

3. The parents' marital relationship may end, but for their children they remain parents always. The only question is whether they will be an involved parent or an absent but fantasied parent.

4. The plan that all family members can devise themselves for custody and access arrangements has a greater chance of success than one that is imposed, whether by a clinician's opinion or through judicial order.

Although these represent impressive progress in understanding between the legal and mental health professions, they represent years of struggle in clarifying professional roles.

For most clinicians, the prospect of including the function of expert witness in their professional role caused deep anxiety. Mental health professionals in forensic psychiatry were called upon for evidence by one lawyer whose responsibility it was to prepare or educate the clinician as to what to expect and what clinical material would likely be required. Clinicians who undertake to work with all family members with regard to a custody and access dispute are in a very different role: the witness of the court or of all involved counsel. As the court's witness, the clinician will likely be under cross-examination by all counsel but with the court holding particular responsibility to ensure that the witness is dealt with fairly and courteously. The more frequent role in our experience has been as an expert witness at the request of all counsel for cross-examination by all. Although the Custody Project members have held to an open mediation-assessment process, only in a small percentage of cases has the request for appearance in court been made. Anxiety about testifying is probably a greater problem than testifying itself. To this end, the training of mental health professionals in providing expert testimony can be useful and reassuring.

On Being an Expert Witness

The Custody Project members have appreciated greatly the assistance of lawyers and judges in providing education in the rules of evidence at a level useful to the layperson. The skills in providing expert testimony are best learned through participation in mock trials or role playing. These require the assistance of a legal colleague. When experiential training is not available, the clinician can gain a better understanding of the court process and the role of the expert witness as described in the literature by several authors. A notable example is the work of Bala and Clarke (1981).

An expert witness has been defined as "one who by *experience* has acquired special or peculiar knowledge of the subject of which he undertakes to testify and it does not matter whether such knowledge has been acquired by study or scientific works or by practical observations" (Rice v. Sockett, 1912, 27 O.L.R. 410, Ont. K.B.). The court must be satisfied that the witness is in fact an expert. This is accomplished through the process of qualifying the witness—that is, by counsel's asking the witness to state the qualifications to be considered as demonstrating special expertise. A concise statement providing the clinician's academic background, work experience, and special training generally suffices. At this point, the witness makes an initial impression, which will contribute to the weight his or her evidence is given by the court. Fumbling or hesitant statements about training and experience do not add to the witness's credibility.

Lawyers and judges are trained to prove or disprove facts; they find the clinician's milieu of soft data alien. The quality of intrafamilial relationships may be described through factual events but cannot be viewed as facts in themselves.

In our experience, it is wise for the expert witness to have previously prepared a clear chronology of clinical contacts with the family members. Although the request, or even subpoena, to appear in court may not include a request for the clinician's chart or notes, this factual chronology is likely to be necessary.

Examination of Expert Witness

When a mental health professional undertakes to give evidence in court, he or she is examined through a three-step process.

Examination-in-Chief

This examination is conducted by the lawyer who has called the expert as a witness, and it is during this examination that the witness should produce all of the evidence in his or her possession. The counsel who is leading the evidence will attempt to ensure this. If the evidence is not disclosed fully at this time, there may not be another chance to do so. This lawyer cannot later bring forth any new evidence, at least not without special leave of the court, which may or may not be granted. It is important for the witness to produce the evidence in a straightforward manner.

Cross-examination

When the examination-in-chief is completed, the other side has the right to cross-examine the witness. This is done by asking more questions. If it can be shown that the witness has lied, exaggerated, or was mistaken or prejudiced, the weight of the witness's previous evidence will be greatly lessened. During cross-examination, counsel may use leading questions, suggestions, or proposals that were not possible for the counsel conducting the examination-in-chief.

It is this stage of cross-examination that raises most anxiety for the mental health professional who has been called as an expert witness. In our view, such anxiety is justified. One concern of most clinicians when giving evidence in a procedure involving a client or patient is that it will not be possible to avoid damaging the therapeutic relationship with the clients, particularly during cross-examination.

The testifying clinician fears that he or she will be pressed to make such negative statements that a later therapeutic relationship is not possible or that cross-examination may result in the clinician's being asked to give information that is a betrayal of the traditional confidentiality between a clinician and a client. In Ontario, until the recently proclaimed Children's Law Reform Act with its provisions for closed mediation, the only inviolable confidentiality or privileged communication has been in the solicitor–client relationship. The clinician–client communication was not inviolate. In our experience, however, if the question posed to the expert witness raises in the clinician's view a serious risk of psychological damage to a family member present in court, it has been possible for the witness to state this and ask direction of the court. The presiding judge may ask that the question be asked in a different way or that a family member, particularly a child, be excused from the hearing, or the judge may request that the witness answer. If the court requires the witness to answer, the witness must comply. It is perhaps helpful to remember that in clinical work, skill has had to be attained in saying sensitive things in a minimally destructive fashion; this is a time to utilize that skill.

A second major concern is the professional's inherent conviction that a major goal of the cross-examination counsel is to discredit or, even worse, to cause the witness to discredit himself or herself by creating contradictions in the evidence as given. This concern may be less realistic. It is based in part in a lack of understanding between professions. Supposedly, the clinician deals with soft data and the lawyer in hard facts. In fact, the difference between them is not great. The thorough clinician has collected many facts and made careful observations, based in a sound theoretical framework, upon which formulation of the case can be made.

Much in the way that therapists have developed a body of knowledge with regard to interviewing techniques, so has the legal profession. The use of the extended rhetorical question and the use by counsel of a warm, supportive approach to lead the witness beyond his or her area of expertise are two interviewing techniques developed by the legal profession for cross-examination. In the process of learning to be an expert witness, it can be reassuring to observe and redefine the cross-examination process in clinical terms.

A real danger for the clinician in providing expert testimony is more likely to be the investment—positive or negative countertransference—that may have developed with regard to the clients. This is particularly true if the mental health professional has undertaken an advocacy role with regard to one family member, most often the child. The ability to be objective in giving assessment information about clients is most severely strained in such a situation. Although the clinical process may have been child focused, the role of advocate for the child is a separate one, carried preferably by a lawyer, not the clinician assessing all family members.

Reexamination

When cross-examination is finished, the lawyer who originally called one as a witness may reexamine for the express purpose of clarifying points brought out or raised during the cross-examination. This segment of examination is available to counsel to clarify to the court some point that has been thought to have been raised incompletely in cross-examination. No new evidence may be brought out during reexamination without the express permission of the court. If such new evidence is brought out with permission, then the opposite side is permitted to re-cross-examine. At any point the court may ask the witness questions.

Witness for the Court

Mental health professionals may be requested by the court to give evidence. This situation frequently exists for those providing clinical services in relation to a custody and access dispute referred at the initiation of the presiding judge. An expert may also be asked to give evidence around a theoretical issue at the court's request.

In such situations, the expert is clearly not a witness for the counsel for just one of the litigants. This is unlike criminal proceedings wherein usually either the crown attorney or the defense counsel calls the expert witness, that lawyer then having a particular investment in providing either some precourt preparation of the witness or, during the proceedings, some protection of the witness. The expert witness who has assessed all family members is more likely to be perceived as a person all counsel wish to cross-examine.

In such situations, the expert witness may feel less protected; however, the presiding judge in all courts has responsibility for ensuring that the proceeding carries forward with fairness and adequate courtesy to all involved. In our experience, there are varying opinions among the judiciary as to whether the court holds any particular responsibility for the witness the court has called. There does seem to be agreement that in such a situation, if the witness has a question, the court is willing to have such a question directed to it.

Useful Expert Witness

When giving evidence in court, the witness should relate in as ordinary language as possible the information that he or she is there to provide. If one is truly expert in the situation that is the subject of the proceeding, one should be able to respond to questions in a straightforward manner.

When asked a question, the expert witness should listen carefully, ensure that the question is understood, and then reply as clearly and simply as is possible. There appears to be considerable temptation on the part of mental health professionals to give prolonged theoretical answers heavily loaded with jargon. One could hypothesize that this brings some kind of reassurance of one's adequacy in an unfamiliar situation; however, it is not usually helpful to the court or counsel and can serve to discredit the expert rather than to increase the weight of his or her opinion. If the witness's knowledge of the area of practice is adequate and the theoretical constructs in which the opinions are based are sound, they can be expressed in everyday language.

In an extended cross-examination, the witness may become weary and even impatient with what appears to be repetitive questioning on an issue that has seemed previously to be dealt with adequately. To become irritable or discourteous is not useful. It is a time to be particularly careful that one understands the question and provides succinct answers.

Perhaps the most useful rule of thumb in providing expert testimony is to remember that no matter how carefully the clinician has undertaken the assessment, it is not possible to know everything. If one does not know the answer to a question, the credible witness so states.

Summary

The roles of psychiatry, social work, and psychology in mental health have developed rapidly over the past century, each affecting the other through their collaboration in the mental hygiene and child guidance movements. Their collaboration with the judicial system developed first in the civil and criminal courts whose adversarial process contrasted with the paternalistic, child-oriented, rehabilitative philosophy of the juvenile courts.

The mental health professional needs to acquire knowledge about the legal profession and the judicial system and a familiarity with the interface between professions. Therapeutic skills must be modified to include a directive and educative approach to parents.

4
Custody Project Model

Robert J. Simmons
Ruth S. Parry

The Custody Project is a group of private practitioners under the aegis of the Child and Adolescent Division of the Department of Psychiatry of the University of Toronto. This professional association was instigated in 1971 by a request for assistance from the judiciary, specifically Mr. Justice Edson Haines of the Supreme Court of Ontario. The project's formation, then, was a response to the external legal and judicial system rather than an intraprofessional response to a perceived need. The Custody Project model, with its strong emphasis on clinician–lawyer cooperation, may have been strongly colored by its origins. Each Custody Project member's primary commitment was to provide clinical services, teaching, and research in one of a number of child psychiatry teaching centers. The project's evolution was affected by each member's obligation to provide leadership in his or her primary setting for training of colleagues and students of various disciplines in guidelines for intervention with families disputing custody and access of their children.

Concurrent with the development of the Custody Project's model, a wide variety of other models for services to families disputing custody and access was developing across North America. To our knowledge, no data are available with regard to the kinds or numbers of models through which mental health professionals provide such services. We believe that the preponderance of services provided in most communities is by individual social workers, psychiatrists, and psychologists as private practitioners. Court-based conciliation and mediation services are increasingly available, usually staffed by a group of counselors available directly to the parents or upon referral by the court or counsel. In some areas utilization of such services is mandatory by statute (Michigan, Child Custody Act, 1970); in others the courts in the initial hearing strongly encourage use by families of conciliation and mediation services prior to further litigation. In some communities, community mental health settings have established special projects or teams to undertake custody and access mediation and assessment services.

Service to separating and divorcing families disputing custody and/or access of their children, whether undertaken by an individual practitioner or group of practitioners, inevitably must address three questions:

1. To whose request for service is the mental health professional responding: the parents', the court's, the lawyer's, the child's, the family's?
2. What clinical process is to be carried out?
3. What techniques of intervention are most effective in settling the dispute and fostering the family members' progress through the separation and divorce process?

This chapter will address the first question; the second will be discussed by Hood (chapter 6) and the last by Broder (chapter 7).

Review of the Literature

Over the past decade, a number of models for services to families disputing custody and/or access have been described in the literature. Benedek and Benedek (1972) were among the first to discuss the question as to whose expert the mental health professional should be. In their experience, the court-appointed psychiatrist or friend of the court had the maximal opportunity for maintaining the required independent and objective role. Families would be referred to the assessor directly by the courts, and assessment findings would be reported directly back to the court. By definition, the families had to have been involved in litigation already. These authors suggest that from this position, the assessor is best able to undertake determination of the custody and/or access dispute. They propose as the guideline for evaluating the best interests of the child the sum of the ten factors included in the Michigan Child Custody Act (1970).

Lewis (1974) discussed three models for mental health professionals in assessment of families disputing custody and/or access: an expert obtained by each party to the dispute, the court-appointed psychiatrist, or a panel of experts from each community. The first option Lewis suggested might increase the possibility of all pertinent information being elicited for the assistance of the court; the second he suggested might result in a judge's appointing an expert whose particular viewpoint might accord with his own, ignoring other responsible experts with differing biases. Lewis encouraged the third option, a panel of experts, although recognizing that a court or the litigants would always retain the right to seek an expert from outside the panel. This author noted the difficulties in formulating a precise standard for what constitutes "the best interests of the child." The needs of a child from birth to three years are viewed as primarily continuity of care and affection. Lewis discusses the needs of the latency child, particularly citing the need for stimulation of intellectual, emotional, and social interests inside and outside the family; the need for an environment that promotes increasing the stability of ego and superego functions and avoids damage through poor impulse control and contradictory identifications; and appropriate disengagement from psychological dependence on the parents. Disruption of continuity of care after the age of seven is seen as not necessarily as harmful as it would be for the younger child.

Levy (1978) and Warner and Elliott (1979) in describing their models also support the concept of a court-appointed assessor. Levy describes an assessment process in which each parent and the child is seen two or three times followed by parent–child interviews and finally a total family interview. Warner and Elliott describe a multidisciplinary team approach at the Denver Colorado Children's Diagnostic Center. Parents are seen by one team member and the child by another as a means of ensuring that the assessor's evaluation of the child is not influenced by the perceived needs of the parents. Recommendations to the court, made after the assessment findings are discussed with the family, or at least the parents, reflect the consensus of the team. The assessment process is completed in one week. Following the termination interview, the center will not be involved in ongoing contact with the family.

Westman (1971) suggests that the mental health professional be appointed by either the court or the guardian ad litem (that is, the person advocating for the child, usually a lawyer). He notes that custody evaluations frequently do not provide information relevant for the court's purposes and suggests that the criteria for evaluation should be similar to those stated in the Michigan Child Custody Act (1970). Westman stresses the changing needs of children at different developmental stages and lists these in six areas: social skills, self-control, ability to learn, values system, ability to make decisions, self-identity, and self-esteem. Recommendations with regard to custody and/or access result from assessment of the child's needs and each parent's ability to meet these.

Solow and Adams (1977) propose a model in which they accept referrals from the guardian ad litem and undertake a strong child advocacy role. They contract with counsel for each parent to undertake binding arbitration. In their view, the judicial opinion is replaced by the mental health professional's, although there is also a report back to court. The contract does not preclude any party from applying to the court at a future date. The assessment process involves all family members. Upon completion, a full report is given to both parents with regard to their child. Assessment findings with regard to the parents are not shared but provided to each parent about himself or herself only.

Kargman (1979) described a model in which she, in the role of guardian ad litem, utilizing her training as a lawyer and as a marriage and divorce counselor, undertakes the assessment. The assessment process includes interviews with both parents jointly in the presence of their counsel and interviews with the children and the parents in the family home regarding the children's wishes as to their own custody and access planning. Other information is collected from community resources that have been previously involved with the children. As a result of this experience, Kargman feels that children should have legal representation and that the role of the guardian ad litem should be studied further. She recommends that counsel for the children remain involved with them as long as they are minors since the court retains jurisdiction throughout that time.

The Group for the Advancement of Psychiatry (1980) strongly recommends a family systems approach to custody evaluation, with a team approach in which one clinician examines the parents and another the child, with both seeing the family together. Referrals to a mental health professional of families conflicted over custody and/or access, they suggest, may be by "an enlightened judge" or a "conscientious attorney." This publication includes a thoughtful outline for the examination of the parents individually, the child individually, the parents in a conjoint interview, and examination of the parent–child interaction. The Group for the Advancement of Psychiatry urges that clinicians undertaking evaluation of custody and access disputes should make every effort to encourage negotiation and compromise among the family members in order to avoid litigation.

Chasin and Grunebaum (1981) describe a model in which the mental health professional is sought by both parents and their lawyers as an impartial evaluator of the entire situation. At times, these authors have undertaken the role of guardian ad litem at the court's request, but even in these instances, they state that it is preferable for this role to be undertaken with the support of the litigants and their lawyers. In this model, the authors request that the parents sign an agreement that outlines the evaluation process and criteria that are to be used in the recommendation resulting from the evaluation. A financial agreement is also made, the authors' preference being that the parents share the costs of the evaluation except in cases in which it would not be equitable for such an arrangement. Fees are paid in advance because Chasin and Grunebaum have found that the parent who is displeased by the findings and recommendations ensuing from the evaluation may be reluctant to carry his or her share of the costs. Although there is no exact formula for the composition and sequencing of the interview process, all family members are interviewed, each parent separately, the children together, and each parent with all of the children, then each parent separately again. These authors also interview other significant persons, such as extended family members, babysitters, friends, and school personnel. If the family can move toward a negotiated settlement or mediated solution, the authors have a series of meetings with the parents and their lawyers. In the parent–child interviews, the authors set out specific tasks through which the nature of the parent–child relationship can be assessed.

Gardner (1982) urges that the mental health professional avoid being the advocate for any family member, seeking only to be as impartial an expert as can be achieved. He notes that this is an ideal and that in reality a clinician's own value system inevitably affects the relationship with all family members, as it does in therapy with adults or children not involved in litigation.

Jackson and colleagues (1980) report a model in which their resource undertakes referrals from the court only and view their position as a neutral party who as an agent of the court is evaluating the child's needs. However, the *resource* is the court's agent, not an individual member of that resource. In this way, the concern raised by Lewis (1974) that the court-appointed psychiatrist model might lead to a court's appointing an assessor that shares the referring judge's own biases is avoided. Jackson and coworkers strongly support a team approach, one in which the parents are seen by one member and the child by another. These authors state that the rationale for this approach is that it ensures greater objectivity by the assessors. In effect, the mental health professionals' investment in or advocacy of either parent or child is contained by the use of more than one clinician. Final recommendations are arrived at by consensus of the clinical team, and these are reported in writing to the court.

Custody Project Model

In responding to the request for clinical services for families disputing custody and access, from 1971 to 1975 a few child psychiatrists in the Child and Adolescent Division of the Department of Psychiatry undertook referrals from the presiding Supreme Court justice. The referrals were subsequent to a judicial order, more accurately described as a referral on consent of the parties facilitated by the court. In Ontario the authority to order a family to be involved in assessment in a family law matter did not exist at that time; however, the court's ability to persuade counsel and the parties of the need for clinical intervention was substantial. At that point, the assessor's role was similar to the court-appointed psychiatrist model. Even at that early stage, however, the court's referral was to a group of private practitioners through the Child Psychiatry Division, not directly to a particular clinician. The referring judge, counsel, all parties, and the clinician agreed that all family members would be involved in the assessment and that a written report would be forwarded to the court and counsel. The report would include the clinician's opinion on custody and/or access arrangements, and he or she would be available to provide expert testimony.

By 1976 there was a sharp increase in referrals, requiring the services of a larger number of mental health professionals. The decision was made that the Family Court Clinic of the Clarke Institute of Psychiatry would undertake administrative responsibility for the program. The Custody Project of the Department of Psychiatry of the University of Toronto was established. The policy that assessments would be undertaken only when all parties to the dispute were in agreement to involve themselves in the assessment was continued.

From their previous experience, the Custody Project members perceived court-initiated referrals as valuable but by definition initiated after litigation had begun. It was hypothesized that this would be months at least after the emotional crisis of separation. On the basis that intervention might be more effective much earlier in the separation process, the members agreed to take referrals initiated by lawyers in the hope that these would be prior to litigation.

Custody Project Structure

From 1976 to 1984, the coordinator of the Custody Project was the director of the Family Court Clinic, assisted by the business administrator of the clinic. The project as an association of academic colleagues providing services to families as private practitioners has no corporate identity in a legal sense. The coordinator's role is to facilitate the evolution of the project in its goals of service, training, and research through its relationships with the Department of Psychiatry as the sponsoring body and with the courts and private bar. The administrator receives referrals, and with the coordinator a screening process is carried out. The administrator ensures that referral procedures are completed.

Participants in the Project

Most of the clinicians are full-time staff of child psychiatry training settings within the University of Toronto; two have part-time appointments. Of the twelve regular participants, most are psychiatrists, two are social workers, and two are psychologists. The contribution of the psychologists has been mainly in research activity or in collaborating in assessments with the other clinicians, who carry basic responsibility for the cases assigned to them.

In their separate child psychiatry teaching centers, all project members have had considerable experience providing assessment and treatment services to children and families involved with the juvenile and child protection courts. Through this, each had gained some knowledge of the interface between the mental health and legal-judicial systems.

Project Meetings

Participants in the project meet twice each month. All project cases are discussed with a view to identifying clinical issues that can be conceptualized into guidelines. In 1979, the development of a data collection instrument was initiated, and subsequently the clinical research was the focus of much of the members' time.

Because of the complexity of custody and access disputes and the lack of experience and research in this area, the project members required support from and consultation with each other. Cases have been discussed both early and late in the clinical process. For example, a new case with unfamiliar problems may require modification of the usual initial intervention.

> *Mr. and Mrs. Bauer had been litigating the access of their three sons for four years. Although Mrs. Bauer had been awarded custody of the children by the court, the oldest boy, Irwin, age fifteen, had refused to remain in her home and was living with Mr. Bauer. Danny, age thirteen, and Stephen, age nine, remained with the mother and her new partner. The specific access arrangements were disrupted by both parents, Irwin and Stephen in their alignment with the father supporting his position, Danny aligned with Mrs. Bauer supporting hers. In the initial meeting with the lawyers, it was learned that Mrs. Bauer's lawyer was her employer. All documentation between her lawyer and Mr. Bauer's lawyer or between the clinician and the lawyers was handled by her before the lawyer saw it.*

Although the clinician could note to both lawyers that the employee–employer relationship of one parent to her legal representative was disruptive to the usual cooperation with counsel, Project Custody staff had no ability to enforce any change by Mrs. Bauer or her lawyer. However, discussion in a project meeting helped in identifying the obstacle this created in the assessment process. On this basis, both counsel were informed that project staff could not continue the assessment unless there was greater clarity between Mrs. Bauer's solicitor–client and employer–employee relationships.

Late in the assessment, the clinician may be unable, in spite of having a great deal of information, to develop clear options with regard to custody and access planning. Presentation in a case conference, often with lively discussion, usually clarifies the difficulties and allows the clinician to reach a conclusion or to undertake further useful clinical activity.

Group discussion provides a check on the development of biases or countertransference reactions by a clinician toward parents or children. Discussion helps to restore objectivity and thus to improve clinical service and the group's understanding of these highly contentious, polarized cases.

The stable composition of the project group over the years has resulted in the members having considerable trust in one another, allowing for a comfortable sharing by each of those clinical dilemmas that are particularly sensitive. The collective experience, review, and feedback provided by the project meetings has improved quality of service, led to development of guidelines for intervention, and raised issues for clinical research.

At times counsel, aware that cases are presented to the project meetings, have expressed concern that opinions and recommendations may be made by the group rather than the individual clinician. The project has been careful to ensure that the clinician is totally responsible for his or her recommendations and thus only he or she is subject to requests for written reports or attendance at court.

Most cases were presented in project meetings at least once, while others required further consultation (table 4–1). Of all the cases, 17 percent were not presented for discussion. Most of these were cases referred prior to the formalizing of the project in 1976 and the initiation of bimonthly meetings. A few were referred late in 1980 when case presentation was limited to particularly complex situations so that time was available in meetings to plan the research study.

In the sharing of clinical dilemmas, growth in the development of techniques and understanding took place within each member. Integration of others' experience and perspective was valuable in helping each clinician's individual approach.

Professional Fees

No funds have been available to the project apart from a nominal administrative fee paid by counsel at the time of referral. Cases have been undertaken as part of each clinician's private practice, and payment of fees is made directly by counsel to the clinician. Early in the project's existence, it was found that in some situations, the contesting parties could not be relied on to pay their agreed portions of the professional fees. It was decided that cases should be

Table 4–1
Number of Times Cases Are Presented

Number of Meetings	Percentage of Cases
0	17
1	71
2	11
3	0
4	1

accepted only with the written undertaking of each counsel for payment of fees, the sharing of costs by the litigants to be negotiated between counsel. This procedure has been successful in ensuring payment and has guaranteed the commitment of counsel and parents to constructive use of the assessment–mediation process. Indeed, without such guarantees of payment, it is unlikely that clinicians would have been able to afford to undertake these complicated and relatively costly assessments. The Ontario Medical Insurance Plan does not cover court-related assessments. Our experience has been similar to that reported by others (Chasin and Grunebaum 1981). Disappointed clients can be reluctant to pay their accounts, and while lawyers can avert this difficulty by requesting a retainer, it was felt that the retainer system is incongruent and ethically questionable in clinical practice. Accounts are submitted to counsel on a monthly basis. Because of the considerable amount of time required for reading of court transcripts and affidavits, for discussion with counsel, writing of the report, and, when necessary, attendance at court, all activity undertaken by the clinician in relation to the case is billed at an hourly rate.

Administrative Operation of the Project

Referrals are received by the project coordinator and administrator and may have been suggested by one or all involved lawyers or the court. For 37 percent of the referrals, more than one source was involved in initiating the request for service. Almost 60 percent of the referrals were initiated by the presiding judge or one of the parents' lawyers (table 4–2).

The project members agreed to accept referrals from lawyers directly in the hope that clinical assistance would be requested more frequently earlier in the families separation process; however, more than three quarters of the families in the study population were referred at some state of litigation, and only a small proportion (23 percent) were direct lawyer-initiated referrals apart from a court proceeding (table 4–3).

Table 4–2
Referral Initiation

Referral Initiator	Percentage of Cases
Judge	28
Father's counsel	17
Mother's counsel	13
Father	4
Mother	0
Official guardian (child's lawyer)	1
Others (including more than one of above)	37

Table 4–3
Referral Source

Source	Percentage of Cases
Motions court	17
Pretrial court	30
Master	5
Trial court	26
No court	23

Although 95 percent of the 116 families in the study population were referred to the project between 1976 and 1980, these data may be a reflection of the project's origin as a response to a request from the judiciary. Throughout the project's life, there has been a consistent rise in lawyer-initiated referrals to the point that in 1979–1980 only 11 percent of the referrals were initiated by the presiding justice. Lawyer-initiated referrals were equally likely to originate with the fathers' or mothers' counsel. Only 1 percent of referrals were initiated by the legal representative for the child from 1976 to 1980. In Ontario, the Office of the Official Guardian is available to the court when there is a perceived need for representation of a child in a custody and access dispute. Following a major study, this provincial resource enlarged its mandate in 1980 to include independent representation of children, particularly those involved in a child protection hearing (Attorney General's Committee on the Representation of Children, 1978). Since that time, representation of children in an intrafamilial dispute has been more frequent, and referrals to the project from the child's counsel have increased.

The project members concur with Gardner (1982) that the impartiality of the clinician is compromised if advocacy of any family member is undertaken. When this appears a likelihood, project staff suggest to both parents' lawyers that they request legal representation for the child. In the rare instances when one counsel has refused the suggestion, project members have made the request directly to the Official Guardian.

In response to a referral inquiry, the project administrator forwards a letter to all counsel in which the Custody Project is described. Questionnaires for completion by each lawyer and his or her client accompany the letter. (See appendix A.) The letter outlines the conditions under which the project will accept a case:

1. All parties to the dispute and counsel agree to the assessment in writing, including the acknowledgment that they are in agreement for the clinician to interview or obtain information from any person perceived as signif-

icant in the situation. Such information is sought only on the basis of the parents' written consent.

2. A nominal administrative fee is required, forwarded by one or both lawyers as determined by them in consultation with their clients.

3. The lawyer and parent questionnaires must be completed in order to provide basic demographic information about the family members, the history of previous litigation, if any, the current legal status, and a statement by each parent as to his or her position with regard to custody, access, or both.

4. Each lawyer is requested to provide a written undertaking for the payment of professional fees, the sharing of these by the parties to the dispute to be arranged between them and their lawyers.

It is made clear in the project's covering letter that the case cannot be assigned to a project member unless the four conditions are met and the requested written material received. These procedures prevent premature clinical activity in situations in which there is no real consensus between the parties to seek clinical assistance as an alternative to litigation. Approximately 15 percent of referrals do not proceed beyond this stage. Others may require some weeks before the conditions of the referral are met, perhaps because of hesitation on the part of counsel or client. When the requested material has been received, often accompanied by copies of petitions, affidavits, reports from the Office of the Official Guardian, and court endorsements, the case is assigned to a clinician.

Increasingly over the years of the project's activity, counsel may request that assignment be to a particular project member, usually on the basis of previous collaboration. As noted in the Final Report of the Toronto Conciliation Project (1980) an important factor in effective lawyer–clinician collaboration has been found to be the depth of their mutual understanding of and trust in one another's roles. Requests by counsel for the services of a specific clinician are accommodated whenever possible.

With transfer of the case material to a clinician, the referral ceases to be an administrative responsibility of the project. The next state of the process is between clinician and counsel. Although the introductory covering letter initially sent to counsel provides a range of professional fees as established by the project members and a range of hours usually required to complete the mediation-assessment process, the clinician at this point is expected to write to all counsel advising them of the specific fee level and provisional estimate of the clinical hours likely to be required in the particular situation based on the written material received. If early in the contact with the family members, it becomes evident that this time estimate must be revised, the clinician is expected to so advise counsel. This is of particular importance in cases in which one or more parties has obtained legal representation with the assistance of the Ontario Legal Aid Plan.

Review of the written material provided by lawyers and their clients at the point of referral may reveal issues that require clarification by counsel before clinical interviews begin. If the lawyers and clinicians have a previous working relationship, this may be done informally by telephone. In the project members' experience, however, it has been useful prior to any contact with family members to arrange a meeting with all counsel. The primary focus is clarification of the roles and expectations of counsel and clinician. Concerns specific to the family may be identified by counsel, providing assistance to the clinician in planning initial contact.

A further advantage in the initial lawyer–clinician meeting lies in the opportunity provided to the clinician to identify particular views on the part of counsel that might unwittingly contribute to the conflict, hinder efforts to engage the family members in a therapeutic alliance, or reduce the clinician's ability to elicit agreement between the parents about a custody and/or access plan. A lawyer who has become personally identified with his or her client's aspirations may be unable to help the client modify this position, and it is useful to understand this process if it has occurred. If the dispute has been through lengthy litigation prior to referral, the lawyers, through previous extensive contact, may have developed some negative views of one another, which can color future negotiations adversely.

Enmeshed in the custody and/or access dispute may be disputes with regard to the matrimonial home, financial assets, and future arrangements for the financial support of the family. Although project members do not undertake mediation-assessment of these matters directly, information about these disputes is valuable to the clinician. Subsequently the clinician's understanding of the emotionality surrounding the property and financial matters can be of help to counsel.

> Both Mr. and Mrs. Gerrard felt firmly that the children should remain in the matrimonial home regardless of which parent was awarded custody. Each felt that the continuity of school placement and neighborhood friends was essential to minimizing the children's distress. In effect, the position of each parent was to win custody of the children and possession of the family home until the youngest child reached age sixteen.

During the clinical work with the family, difficulty may arise in gaining written consent for release of information from an important, previously utilized community resource. Lawyers have a long tradition in control of the client. The lawyer's assistance in gaining the client's cooperation may be needed by the clinician if the assessment is not to flounder.

Each lawyer has a specific obligation to the client: protecting the client's rights. As the clinical understanding of the family develops, it has been found useful to meet with counsel again to provide some information as to the direction the family members appear to be taking in developing a plan of their own. In more intractable situations, mediation may not be possible, and work with the family may have to result in an opinion and recommendations with regard to the custody and/or access arrangements that would be given to the family, counsel, and, if necessary, to the court. Counsel need to understand this in order to conduct their case. In the most contentious situations, a meeting with counsel with regard to the clinician's opinion and recommendations is mandatory; frequently it is followed immediately by a joint conference with the conflicting parents and their lawyers.

In the 116 cases comprising this study population, lawyer-clinician contact by telephone calls, letters, and conferences varied greatly, in general increasing over the project's life. The majority of cases included several telephone calls and two or more letters, and almost half included one conference at least. Project members were meticulous in maintaining equal contact with all lawyers involved with one family. Prior to the final written report, no information was given to either parent's lawyer about the other parent. Occasionally if there was deep concern about one parent's emotional state or potential for violence, the clinician would discuss this with that person's lawyer, usually to coordinate efforts in seeking psychiatric assistance for the client independent from the Custody Project clinician's involvement.

The importance of close cooperation between the clinician and all involved lawyers cannot be overstated. This professional alliance is essential if the clients are to be helped to redirect their efforts from an acrimonious competition to a more constructive focus: the real needs and circumstances of their children and themselves.

5

Family Characteristics and Clinical Interventions in Custody and/or Access Disputes: The Data

Elisabeth B. Saunders

Methods of therapeutic interventions develop as a result of the interaction between the therapist's theoretical and clinical orientation and the particular characteristics and needs of the patient population seen. In chapter 3 the theoretical and clinical evolution of the mental health professions, their coming together in an interdisciplinary team as a result of the child guidance movement, and their involvement as clinical resources in various kinds of court actions, including family disputes, was described. Chapter 4 discusses the specific kind of training and clinical orientation that members of the Custody Project brought with them when they met the first families referred because of an ongoing custody dispute over ten years ago.

Since then the Custody Project members have had to reevaluate and modify the theoretical and clinical principles that they brought to these families and develop new methods of working with the problems they presented. Throughout this process, the clinicians formulated ideas about the characteristics of parents who remain locked into lengthy, costly, acrimonious custody and/or access disputes that persisted in spite of interventions by the legal system and often by clinicians as well.

The next step was to find a way to investigate systematically these observations. The aim of this chapter is threefold:

1. To describe the method of data collection developed for this study.
2. To describe the characteristics of the families seen as part of the Custody Project and how they may have affected the development of clinical methods.
3. To discuss the limitations of our research and present suggestions for future research that emerged as we struggled with our frustration about the questions our data could not answer.

Families and Custody Decisions: Issues of Research Methodology

Families who are caught in a custody dispute and who come to the attention of clinicians are a subgroup of separating families. Separating families can follow one or more of several possible pathways in order to decide the issue of custody of minor children. Some families never face a custody dispute, perhaps because one parent does not want custody and the other obtains it by default. Other parents struggle with the question of custody but are able to resolve it on their own or with the help of their lawyers and/or the court. Another group of parents turns to mental health professionals for help in resolving the issue of custody. Nobody knows what percentage of separating families falls into any of these groups. Further, these subgroups of separating families are heterogeneous themselves. Thus families come to the legal as well as the mental health professions at different points in the separating process, requiring different kinds of services and interventions. When we consider only the subgroup that comes to the attention of mental health professions, several subclassifications immediately come to mind, differing in the way in which they come to the clinician, in the length of time between the separation and contact with a clinician, and in the kind of clinical services provided (Benedek and Benedek 1979).

In the literature such distinctions among subgroups are rarely, if ever, made. Instead researchers investigating the effects of various kinds of custody and access arrangements on children and their parents and clinicians discussing methods of assessment and intervention in custody disputes usually describe the families as if they were a homogeneous group. This is a serious limitation since the research and clinical literature on the effects of divorce on children, which is really research on children growing up in their mother's custody, has already shown at least these children to be a heterogenous group. Factors such as maternal adjustment, parenting style, sex of the child, age of the child at the time of separation, and the nature of the relationship between the parents and between the child and the father all influence these children's short-term and sometimes also long-term development (Hetherington, Cox, and Cox 1978; Levitin 1979; Longfellow 1979). Indeed these factors may be more influential than is the nature of the custody arrangement by itself (Levitin 1979; Santrock and Warshak 1979).

In studies that compare the effects on children of different types of custody arrangements but that do not control for the reasons that the children were placed with one parent rather than the other, there is the implicit assumption that these reasons and the factors contributing to them are identical across all custody arrangements. Such an assumption does not appear to be supportable. It is well known, for example, that fathers are less likely to apply for custody of their children than are mothers and that judges may use different considerations in awarding custody to the mother than they do in awarding custody to the fathers (Gersick 1979; Lowery 1981).

Further, parents who use a joint custody arrangement may have a different kind of relationship with each other than do parents who, as a result of a bitterly contested custody dispute, find themselves with a court order awarding custody to one parent. Children's access to their noncustodial parent can differ widely both within each subgroup of custody arrangements (mother custody, father custody, or joint custody) and among these groups, which in turn may affect parents' and children's satisfaction with their custody arrangement and their reactions to it.

Clinical studies have described various models, approaches, and styles of working with separated families regarding a custody dispute. This literature is helpful to clinicians in showing them the thinking and experience of fellow clinicians struggling with what appears to be the same kind of issues. Indeed, there often is consensus of opinion among clinicians on at least some aspects of working with these families. These clinical studies, however, share the same shortcomings that afflict much other clinical research and have been summarized quite succinctly by Levitin (1979, p. 3) in a review of research on children of divorce:

> For example, the samples are often small, self-selected, and biased in unknown ways. Data based on clinical impressions and insights of one investigator are not easily replicable by other investigators. Many issues of the reliability and validity of the measures remain unresolved. . . . Published articles often fail to describe the sample on which the conclusions are based and readers may need to be reminded that caution must be used in generalizing beyond the children presented in the particular study.

Although these are valid criticisms, separating families and clinicians seeing them regarding a custody or access dispute cannot await well-designed, replicated findings to guide them, and much clinical work probably will always remain outside the realm of hard science.

This books shares some of the shortcomings of clinical publications described by Levitin. Although the sample is self-selected, readers are provided with a detailed description of the sample on which clinical conclusions are based, including the background of the families and their situation at the time of assessment. The nature of the clinical work done with them also is described. Thus the extent to which the observations and assessment and intervention methods described here may be generalized can be ascertained by comparing the characteristics of these families with those of other families caught in custody and/or access disputes and by investigating the applicability of the clinical methods described here to other families caught in a custody and/or access dispute.

The data presented have been obtained by means of a questionnaire, which can be readily used by other investigators. At the present time, some of the authors of this book (Hood, Parry, and Saunders) are using a slightly modified version of this questionnaire to gather more data and investigate the replicability of the observations and data presented here.

Method

A questionnaire was developed to collect data on 116 families seen over a period of nine years by ten clinicians, two of whom are no longer members of the Custody Project. All current Custody Project members participated in the research endeavor.

The clinicians routinely obtain detailed information about the families' presenting problems, the history of their involvement with the legal system, the parents' and children's individual histories, and the parents' marital history. This information is usually summarized in some detail in a lengthy, written report to the referring judge and/or lawyers. For accounting purposes, each clinician keeps a written record of all interviews, telephone contacts, meetings with lawyers, and court appearances. These were favorable conditions to obtain uniform data on the families seen. All that needed to be done was to design a questionnaire that clinicians could use to code the information available to them in such a way that the data could be entered into the computer for storage and data analysis. The questionnaire specified for most questions which source of information was to be used: parents' report, reports by other agencies, or clinician's observations. Current members of the Custody Project completed questionnaires on their own cases. The cases of two previous members were completed in consultation with them.

The reliability of the questionnaire was ascertained in another study, which showed interrater agreement to be .89 (Parry, Hood, and White 1978).

Since nearly all questionnaire items deal with descriptive data referring to demographic kinds of information, validity here means face validity—for example, the validity of the item asking for the level of the father's income is the father's income. These data have face validity as long as they are reliably recorded. Items that asked for an evaluation (for example, of the parents' childhood) were not independently validated. Whenever possible, two sources of information were used for these items, such as parents' self-reports and clinicians' evaluations. These data are considered to have face validity only: to refer to the parents' self-reports and clinicians' evaluations without claiming to be an assessment of what these parents' childhood may have been like.

The Families: Demographic Characteristics

Data were collected on 116 families, 95 percent of them seen in the years 1976 through 1981. Two hundred fifteen children under the age of sixteen were the focus of the custody and/or access dispute. All but one of the couples were the biological parents of the children who were the objects of the dispute. The one couple were adoptive parents.

Over 50 percent of the parents were Canadian born. The others came from all areas of the world, including Europe, South and Central America, the West Indies, Asia, and Australia. Among the immigrant families, most had been living in Canada for over ten years; only a few had been there for fewer than five years. About three-quarters of the parents were residing in the metropolitan Toronto area at the time of the assessment. About 50 percent of the parents were Protestant, a third were Roman Catholic, and the others were about equally distributed among the following religions: Greek Orthodox, Jewish, Hindu, Islam, and no religion. These statistics indicate no over-representation of ethnic families or of any religious group as compared to the metropolitan Toronto population.

For the great majority of the parents (close to 90 percent), this had been their first marriage.

The majority of the parents were in their late twenties or thirties. Fathers were older than mothers, their mean age being thirty-seven as compared to thirty-three for the mothers, a statistically significant difference ($p < .001$). The age range was twenty to fifty years for the mothers and twenty-three to fifty-four for the fathers.

No statistics are available on the age distribution of separating parents. The only data that could be used for comparison purposes show the age distribution of divorcing couples (table 5–1).

Table 5–1
Age at Separation or Divorce

Age[a]	National Statistics, Canada		Custody Project	
	Wife	Husband	Wife	Husband
15–19	1.2%	.2%	0%	9%
20–29	37.8	29.8	29	13
30–39	28.9	35.5	57	54
40–49	18.6	21.4	14	28
50 or over	13.5	13.1	1	4

Source: For national statistics, Statistics Canada 1983. Data are for age of divorcing couples, 1969–1979.

[a]Age at time of assessment.

Custody Project parents were underrepresented in the twenty to twenty-nine years age bracket and overrepresented in the thirty to thirty-nine years age bracket as compared to Canadian national statistics. They were also underrepresented in the fifty and over age bracket, which may be a function of many parents of this age no longer having dependent children to care for.

Following separation, women are more likely to experience a significant drop in income than are men (Ambert 1980; Brandwein, Brown, and Fox 1974). Also among Custody Project families, women tended to have less income than men, although there was a wide range of income levels among both the men and the women. The mean annual income of fathers was $20,582; mothers' mean reported annual earnings were only $9,465. Using t test statistics, this difference was significant at the $p < .001$ level.

The difference in income level between mothers and fathers was due to differences in employment patterns rather than to differences in levels of education. About a third of mothers and fathers had a high school education, another third had obtained some training beyond high school, and a quarter had attained a university education either at the undergraduate or graduate level. Ten percent of the parents had completed only a few grades of elementary school. A chi-square analysis showed significant differences ($p < .001$) in the occupational patterns among mothers and fathers. While the majority of both mothers and fathers were working at the point of referral to the Custody Project, the percentage of parents without paid employment was 8 percent of the fathers but 26 percent of the mothers. Fathers were also more likely to hold managerial or professional positions than were mothers (34 percent of the fathers versus 6 percent of the mothers).

There was no significant difference in the marital status of the mothers and fathers in this study population at the time of the assessment. About two-thirds of the parents were single; the others were either living in a common-law union or were remarried. About 25 percent of the couples had obtained a legal divorce at the time of the assessment.

Legal Proceedings

One way in which the families seen as part of the Custody Project differ from the majority of separated families with children lies in the length of time in which they have been entangled in legal proceedings regarding their separation and regarding issues of custody and/or access. Canadian national statistics indicate that 86 percent of divorce proceedings by parents with children are resolved in less than a year. Less than 3 percent of these families continue court actions for more than two years. Only 52 percent of the Custody Project families had been involved in legal actions for less than a year by the time of their referral. Among the remaining 48 percent of families, 16 percent had been carrying out legal proceedings for more than three years.

Virtually all parents had retained legal counsel for the purpose of these proceedings. In view of the lengthy period of time counsel had been involved with their clients prior to referral to the Custody Project, emphasis on collaboration with the legal profession can be easily understood. These lawyers' assessments of their clients and their problems, their investment in them, and their own views as to how this conflict should be resolved could not be overlooked if one hoped that these lawyers would make appropriate use of the clinical work.

Another outstanding characteristic of the legal dispute is the forcefulness with which the fathers were pursuing custody and/or access to their children. Fifty-one percent of the fathers were the petitioners in the court action that brought the family to the Custody Project. Canadian national statistics indicate that less than a third of fathers with dependent children act as petitioners in a divorce action (Statistics Canada 1983). It is usually the mother who approaches the court as a petitioner (in two-thirds of divorce proceedings involving children), and in only 16 percent of cases are answers or counterpetitions filed. In comparison, in the Custody Project families counterpetitions were filed in three-quarters of cases. Even when the fathers were not initiating the court action, they were actively fighting it with a counterpetition signficantly more often than is true for most separated fathers of dependent children.

The Parents

Who these parents are and why they remain entangled in such protracted custody and/or access disputes is the obvious next question.

Marriage Breakdown: The Social and Cultural Context

The rate of divorce in the Western world has been rising dramatically since the 1960s. Canadian and U.S. statistics indicate that about 40 percent of marriages end in divorce (Hetherington, Cox, and Cox 1978; Statistics Canada 1983). These data could be reflecting cultural changes that have instilled carefree attitudes toward marriage. What once was seen as a bond to be honored for "better for worse," "until death do us part," is now considered only a temporary arrangement to be ended when it has become less than fully satisfactory to one or the other partner. Some believe that the culture of the 1960s and 1970s has fostered the pursuit of individual happiness and immediate need gratification at the expense of lasting commitments (Lasch 1979). Others have not found that parents, particularly of dependent children, end

Table 5–2
Duration of Marriage

Years	Custody Project	National Statistics, Canada[a]
Fewer than 5	22%	24%
5–10	35	31
More than 10	43	46

[a]Statistics Canada 1983. These data are based on 1979 figures, which were calculated on the basis of the date the divorce petition was filed.

their marital relationships easily. Hetherington, Cox, and Cox (1978) observed that divorce constitutes a crisis and that there are no victimless divorces. Wallerstein and Kelly (1980) described parents who have endured long-term marital problems and even abuse before deciding to end their marriage. The Custody Project parents too did not end their marriages quickly or easily.

Although for nearly 50 percent of the couples, marital difficulties began within the first year of their marriage, all but 1 percent remained in their marriages for many years. About a third were married for five to ten years, and over 40 percent had been married for more than ten years by the time of the final separation. About a fifth of the couples separated within the first five years of their marriage. A comparison with Canadian national statistics shows that this distribution of duration of marriage is similar to that found in the population at large (table 5–2).

Another indicator that these couples did not make the decision to separate quickly or easily is the prevalence of previous separations followed by attempts to reconcile with the resumption of cohabitation. In the majority of cases (69 percent), there had been previous separations and reconciliations before at least one partner felt that the marriage was not salvageable. Even at the time of the assessment, 19 percent of the fathers, but only 3 percent of the mothers, indicated that they would like to reconcile with their former spouse.

In about three-quarters of the families, the mother initiated the final separation and left the matrimonial home. It could be speculated that the changing social and cultural climate of the 1970s permitted these women to leave their unhappy marriages.

Intergenerational Transmission of Marital Instability

Another hypothesis regarding the characteristics of the Custody Project parents that may be related to the breakdown of their marriages was derived from the theory of intergenerational transmission of marital instability

(Goode 1971; Kulka and Weingarten 1979). According to this theory, for which there exists supporting empirical evidence, separated or divorced adults are more likely to have experienced the separation of their own parents during their childhood or adolescence than are married, never separated adults.

Close to 40 percent of the fathers and a third of the mothers had experienced a separation from a parent during their childhood or adolescent years. (Only separations lasting more than six months are included in these data.) Custody Project parents were more likely to have been separated from their fathers than their mothers, and the separations from either parent occurred at all age levels.

A significantly ($p < .05$) larger proportion of mothers than of fathers described their childhood as unhappy (18 percent of the fathers, as compared to 37 percent of the mothers). The clinicians believe that many of the parents they were seeing were trying to portray their childhood as having been better than it probably was. Twice as many clinicians as fathers reported that the father had experienced an unhappy childhood (37 percent of the clinicians). In the clinicians' eyes also, the mothers were underreporting the difficulties of their childhood. They stated that in their opinion, 50 percent, not 37 percent, of the mothers had lived through an unhappy childhood. The parents may have been trying to gloss over the difficulties of their childhood since during a custody assessment, parents usually realize that they need to be seen as stable people who can be appropriate role models for their children. Coming from a poor childhood often is seen as a stigma. On the other hand, clinicians may have been overstating the degree of childhood unhappiness in trying to deduce the stresses that their clients were not reporting. Further, trained to recognize psychopathology even where others may not see it, they may have been assuming greater disturbance in these parents' background than there was. If we therefore assume that the truth lies somewhere in the middle between the parents' and the clinicians' reports, then about 25 percent of the fathers and slightly over 40 percent of the mothers had experienced unhappy childhoods.

Twenty-four percent of the fathers and 32 percent of the mothers described their parents' marriage as having been unhappy. In the opinion of the clinicians, these data also underrepresent the number of parents who had witnessed their own parents struggling within an unhappy marriage. According to the clinicians, a third of the fathers and close to half of the mothers had parents whose marriages had been poor.

Separation from one's parents, an unhappy childhood, and an unhappy marriage of one's parents often are not independent of each other. Having parents whose marriage is unhappy increases a child's risk for having an unhappy childhood and experiencing a separation from a parent. Data analysis showed that an unhappy childhood was more often related to an unhappy

Table 5–3
Parents Who Had an Unhappy Childhood

	Self-Report		Clinician's Report	
	Father	*Mother*	*Father*[a]	*Mother*[a]
Separation from a parent	42%	43%	52%	43%
No separation from a parent	58	57	48	57
Parents had unhappy marriage	73	72	88	76
Parents had happy marriage	27	28	12	24

[a]These data refer to clinicians' reports that their clients had an unhappy childhood and clinicians' evaluations of the marriages of clients' parents.

marriage of the parents than was the experience of a separation from a parent. About three-quarters of the Custody Project parents who had experienced an unhappy childhood also had parents whose marriage was unhappy. In comparison only about 40 percent of these parents (Custody Project parents who had unhappy childhoods) had experienced a separation from a parent (see table 5–3).

It may be that these Custody Project fathers and mothers who felt that they suffered an unhappy childhood seeing their own parents locked in an unhappy marriage were seeking to protect their children by ending their own unsatisfactory marriages. Although they had done no better than their parents in trying to find marital happiness, they may have at least wanted to spare their children witnessing the same kinds of marital fights that had frightened them as children.

Parental Characteristics and Marriage Breakdown

Studies of marital adjustment and its relationship to spouses' demographic and personal characteristics have identified subgroups based on the likelihood of their marriages ending in divorce. Couples who marry in their teens and couples whose marriage was forced by an unplanned pregnancy (and there is overlap between the two groups) are two such subgroups at higher risk to end their marriage through a divorce than is true of couples who marry later in their lives and postpone having children for a few years after establishing a marital relationship (Ambert 1980; Statistics Canada 1983). Statistics also indicate that couples who marry soon after meeting each other are another high risk group for divorce. In view of these data, it was expected that many of the Custody Project parents had entered into marriage at a young age, having known each other for a short period of time, and that many married because a baby was on the way.

Table 5–4
Age at Marriage

| Age | Custody Project | | Age | National Statistics, Canada | |
	Fathers	Mothers		Husbands	Wives
Under 19	4%	24%	Under 20	13%	42%
19–25	57	59	20–24	54	41
25 and over	40	17	25 and over	33	17

Source: Statistics Canada 1983 for national Canadian statistics.
[a]These data refer to divorcing spouses only but are not limited to parents.

Age at Marriage

The age at marriage of the Custody Project parents was compared to national statistics regarding the distribution of age at marriage of divorcing husbands and wives (table 5–4). Since the age groupings used in this study and in the Canadian Statistics survey are somewhat different and since the Canadian national data include parents as well as childless divorcing couples, table 5–4 serves as only a rough way of comparing the age at marriage of this sample to the best national data available. With this limitation in mind, it still appears that the Custody Project parents had not married at a young age more often than is true of most divorcing couples.

Length of Courtship

Close to a quarter of the couples had known each other for fewer than six months by the time or their wedding. Another third married within a year following their meeting. Thus about 50 percent of the couples had made a decision to marry within a few months of knowing each other if we assume that usually there is at least a span of several weeks between the time of engagement and the wedding day. Although no national data were found with which these figures could be compared, it appears that for many of these couples, the decision to marry may have been made too hastily, particularly in view of the later course of their marriages.

Premarital Pregnancy

Close to a quarter of the mothers were pregnant before the wedding date. No comparable national statistics were found. Women who married in their teens were somewhat more likely to have been pregnant prior to their marriage than were women marrying at a later age. Forty percent of the mothers

Table 5–5
Onset of Marital Problems

Duration of Marriage[a]	Father's Report	Mother's Report
Less than 1 year	42%	54%
1–4 years	36	27
5–9 years	16	13
10 or more years	6	6

[a]Until separation.

who had married in their teens (under the age of twenty) had been pregnant prior to the wedding.

Husbands' and Wives' Perceptions of Their Marital Difficulties

Husbands and wives often had very different recollections of their life together. For the majority of couples, marital difficulties began in the first five years of their marriage (table 5–5). The spouses stated a wide range of reasons for the breakdown of their marriages, and often there was only partial agreement between husbands and wives as to the nature of their marital difficulties.

In close to half of the families, issues regarding child rearing, money, sexual problems, or the emotional instability of one partner were mentioned by at least one parent. The husband's dissatisfaction with his wife's sexual affairs and her social activities or the wife's dissatisfaction with the husband's social activities were marital problems in close to 40 percent of the couples. In about a quarter of the families, each of the following marital problems was listed: interference by in-laws, husband's long work hours, and husband's extramarital affairs. For about a fifth of the couples, the husband's drinking problem was a source of marital difficulties. Various other problems were mentioned by less than 10 percent of the couples, including religious and social class differences, drug abuse by one partner, the wife's work, drinking problems and/or poor housekeeping, the husband's lack of involvement with his wife and children, husband's unemployment, or differences in life-styles and interests.

Rate of agreement between the spouses as to the nature of their marital difficulties was quite low, ranging from none of the couples agreeing on an issue to a high of 28 percent of couples agreeing that they had differences regarding a particular issue (in this case, child rearing). Out of a list of nineteen possible problem areas, there was agreement between the father and mother in 10 percent or more of the couples on only six issues: child rearing,

Table 5–6
Parents' Reports of Marital Problems

	Both Parents	Neither Parent	Father Only	Mother Only
Child rearing	28%	52%	9%	10%
Sex	20	59	7	14
Money	19	55	8	17
Wife's social activities	15	60	23	2
Husband's work	10	73	2	14
Husband's social activities	10	64	3	22

Table 5–7
Complaints Most Often Mentioned

By Husbands		By Wives	
Wife's social activities	38%	Child rearing	38%
Child rearing	37	Money	36
Wife's affairs	37	Sex	34
Wife's instability	29	Husband's social activities	32
Money	27	Husband's family	26
Sex	27	Husband's work hours	24
Wife's family	23	Husband's affairs	23
Husband's social activities	14	Husband's instability	20
Husband's work hours	12	Husband's drinking	19
		Wife's social activities	16

sexual problems, money, wife's social activities, husband's work, and husband's social activities (table 5–6).

There were also differences in the frequency with which husbands and wives mentioned the various marital problems they encountered (table 5–7). Husbands most often complained about their former wives' social activities, child-rearing practices, their extramarital affairs and instability, money and sexual problems, and interference by their in-laws. Wives most often complained about their husbands' social activities, interference by their in-laws, the husbands' long work hours, their extramarital affairs, emotional instability, drinking problem, and the husbands' disapproval of their (the wives') social activities.

It is tempting to speculate on how the complaints expressed by these spouses about each other may be related to the intensity of their custody dispute. For many of the husbands, acquiescing to their former wives' wish for custody would mean agreeing to give over their children to a woman they see as emotionally unstable, with questionable child-rearing practices, and with an inappropriate social life, which includes sexual affairs. For many of the wives, giving up their battle for custody could mean leaving their children in the care of fathers who are seen to have questionable child-rearing practices, inappropriate social activities, which include sexual affairs, who work long hours, are emotionally unstable, or have a drinking problem. It is not easy for a parent to overcome such concerns about the other parent and come to an agreement regarding the upbringing of the children.

Psychiatric History

The frequency with which the issue of emotional instability of the other spouse was mentioned raises the question whether there is a significant percentage of psychiatrically disturbed people in this group of parents. It appears that many of these parents were rightly concerned about the mental health of their former spouse.

These parents' intense emotionality, their hostility toward the former spouse with the accompanying complaints, accusations, and distorted perceptions of him or her, their inability to let go of the legal actions and negotiate an agreement in spite of the high costs to themselves and their families, both emotionally and financially, created the impression of a psychiatrically disturbed group of people. Thus, one of our hypotheses was that among the Custody Project parents, there would be an overrepresentation of psychiatrically disturbed men and women as compared to available epidemiological statistics.

The issue of psychiatric diagnoses in evaluating parents regarding a custody dispute is complex and sensitive. In the opinion of some clinicians, the use of psychiatric diagnoses, with all their known limitations, is particularly disadvantageous in custody disputes since diagnoses by themselves are not likely to resolve the dispute, while they do open a way for attorneys to discredit the clinician's recommendations by exposing the problematic aspects of psychiatric diagnoses (Gardner 1982). While on the basis of such considerations clinicians do not include psychiatric diagnoses in their reports, Custody Project clinicians concur with Gardner (1982) that an evaluation of the existence of psychopathology in the parents or children is an important part of assessing parenting capacity and the children's functioning and possibly special needs. Thus Custody Project clinicians routinely obtained past psychiatric evaluations if any of the family members had previous contact with mental health professionals, and if they did not record a formal diagnosis, they at least summarized their assessment of the parents' and children's functioning in such a way as to allow a deduction as to whether or what kind of a diagnosis was applicable. The data reported here are based on clinicians' reports of the parents' past contacts with mental health professionals and their diagnoses using the DSM III (Diagnostic and Statistic Manual of Mental Disorders-III, 1980).

Table 5–8
Psychiatric Treatment

| | Custody Project | | U.S. Statistics | |
	Hospitalizations	OPD	Hospitalizations	OPD
Men	7%	34%	2%	2%
Women	14	47	1	2

Source: U.S. statistics based on data reported by Bloom, White, and Asher 1979.
Note: OPD = Outpatient department.

Past Contacts with Mental Health Professionals. Epidemiological studies have shown that separated or divorced adults have higher rates of admission into psychiatric hospitals or clinics for inpatient and for outpatient treatment than do married adults (Bloom, White, and Asher 1979). Therefore, in order to ascertain whether the Custody Project parents had an unusually high incidence of contacts with either inpatient or outpatient treatment facilities, statistics regarding admission rates for psychiatric treatment for separated adults were used for comparative purposes. The ideal comparison group would have been separated parents' rates of mental health contacts, but no such statistics could be found. Custody Project parents had higher rates of admissions for inpatient psychiatric treatment, as well as higher rates of mental health contacts on an outpatient basis than would be predicted based on U.S. survey studies of utilization of inpatient and outpatient psychiatric treatment facilities by separated adults (table 5–8).

As could be expected, there was some overlap between the group of parents who had been hospitalized and the group of parents who had received outpatient treatment. Fifty-four percent of the mothers and 39 percent of the fathers had mental health contacts prior to their referral to the Custody Project. The majority of these treatment contacts occurred while the parents were still living together (table 5–9).

One interpretation of these data would suggest that these parents did not enter their relationship while suffering from psychiatric problems to the extent that they would require or seek out on their own psychiatric treatment, but that during the course of the marriage, they developed symptoms distressing enough to bring them to the attention of treatment facilities. Whether the nature of the marital relationship created or precipitated the disturbance or whether the development of a psychiatric disturbance was a cause of or contributed to the marital breakdown cannot be ascertained by these data alone.

Among the fathers who had been in psychiatric treatment, 50 percent had been seen because of marital problems; the others had presented with a variety of disturbances, including alcohol abuse, depression, neuroses,

Table 5–9
Psychiatric Treatment Contacts

	Previous to the Union	During Union	Following Separation	Total[a]
Psychiatric hospitalizations				
Fathers	2%	6%	0%	7%
Mothers	0	10	7	14
Outpatient mental health contacts				
Fathers	2	28	12	34
Mothers	2	36	21	47

[a]Refers to the percentage of parents who had any kind of psychiatric contact. Since some parents had been in treatment at more than one time and some had been in inpatient as well as in outpatient treatment, the total is smaller than the number of all treatment contacts.

Table 5–10
Reasons for Psychiatric Treatment

	Fathers		Mothers	
	N	%	N	%
Marital problems	22	50	34	61
Alcoholism	6	14	2	4
Depression	5	11	10	18
Suicidal state	3	7	7	12
Neurotic problems	1	2	2	4
Personality disorder problems	5	11	0	0
Psychiatric episode	2	5	1	1
Missing data	2	5	3	5
	44	100	56	100

personality disorder, and psychosis. Among the mothers who had received psychiatric treatment, 61 percent had presented with marital problems and the others with symptoms of alcohol abuse, depression, suicidal states, neurotic problems and psychotic episodes (table 5–10).

Psychiatric Diagnoses. The clinicians used the *Diagnostic and Statistical Manual of Mental Disorders* (Third Edition) in their assessment of the presence of psychiatric disorders among the parents (American Psychiatric Association 1980). According to the DSM-III, a diagnosis can be made on one of two axes. Axis I describes clinical syndromes, for example, organic mental disorders, and "conditions not attributable to a mental disorder that are a focus of attention or treatment," for example, marital problems (American Psychiatric Association 1980). Axis II describes personality disorders and specific developmental disorders.

Using *Axis I* and *II* of the DSM-III, 59 percent of the parents were assigned a psychiatric diagnosis. Fathers and mothers were equally likely to be seen as showing signs of a psychiatric disturbance. In the majority of families (72 percent), at least one parent was seen as psychiatrically disturbed.

On Axis I, a wide range of diagnoses was assigned without any diagnostic category being used more often than the others. The psychiatric disturbances seen in these parents ranged from schizophrenia and major affective disorders to neurotic kinds of disorders, alcohol abuse, mild mental retardation, and transient adjustment disorders reactive to the present crisis. These latter disturbances were expected to be overcome once the current difficulties were resolved.

There is also great variability among the personality disorders diagnosed on Axis II, with no particular category being used significantly more often than the others.

There was no complete overlap between the group of parents who had contact with mental health professionals prior to their referral to the Custody Project and the group of parents assigned a psychiatric diagnosis by the Custody Project clinicians. In other words, Custody Project clinicians did not assign a psychiatric diagnosis to all parents who had a previous mental health contact. Among the mothers who were seen as showing no signs of a psychiatric disturbance, close to 50 percent had seen a mental health professional in the past, usually (in over 60 percent of the cases) regarding marital problems. The data are somewhat different for the fathers. The majority of fathers (72 percent) who were not showing signs of a psychiatric disturbance at the time of the assessment also had no previous mental health contacts. Further, virtually all the fathers who were not given a psychiatric diagnosis but who had past mental health contacts had been seen because of their marital problems. It is tempting to speculate about this difference. One possible interpretation would be that more mothers than fathers sought treatment for transient disturbances that were overcome in the course of treatment, while the majority of fathers who had sought treatment for other than marital problems had presented with disturbances that persisted in spite of treatment.

The Children

The majority of the families (70 percent) had one or two children, with the size of the families ranging from one to ten children. Not all these children were minor (under the age of sixteen) and affected by the custody and/or access dispute. Two hundred and fifteen of these children, however, were the focus of their parents' dispute, and the data presented here refer to these children.

Fifty-eight percent of the children were boys; 42 percent were girls. A quarter were infants and preschoolers, 45 percent were latency-age children,

Table 5–11
Number of Children by Age and Sex in Custody Project

	Age			
	0–5	*6–10*	*11–15*	*N*
Boys	29	57	38	124
Girls	25	39	27	91
	54	96	65	215

(age six to ten), and the remaining 30 percent were between eleven and fifteen years old (table 5–11).

Marital conflicts and the continuation of parents' hostility toward each other following their separation are stressful for children and often result in emotional maladjustment (Herzog and Sudia 1973; Hetherington 1979; Levitin 1979). Since the parents of all children in this sample had unhappy, conflictual marriages and continued to fight with each other following their separation, their children were a high-risk group for the development of symptoms of maladjustment. A third of them showed signs of emotional problems. In addition, a small percentage of school-age children were delinquent or truant. Boys were more likely to show signs of problems of adjustment than were girls (39 percent of the boys as compared to 24 percent of the girls; $p < .05$). This observation is consistent with the findings of other studies that have shown boys to be more adversely affected by their parents' separation than girls (Hetherington, Cox, and Cox 1978). There was no difference between boys and girls regarding their likelihood of showing delinquent or truant behavior, which is mainly due to the incidence of those problems being very low in both groups. Overall 39 percent of the boys and 24 percent of the girls showed signs of emotional problems, delinquent behavior, or truancy.

Custody Recommendations

Numerous considerations enter into making a recommendation regarding custody of a child. Here some statistical relationships between kinds of custody recommendations made and sex of the parent, sex and age of the child, and clinicians' stated reasons for making a specific custody recommendation will be presented. (The meaning of these considerations and the ways in which they influence clinicians' decision making is discussed in depth and illustrated by case examples in chapter 8.)

Table 5–12
Custody Recommendations

	Custody Project	Ontario Statistics
Custody arrangement		
Sole custody	73%	84%
Split custody	18	2
Joint custody	4	n.a.
Other	5	14
Sole custody and recommendations, by sex of parents[a]		
Father	51	14
Mother	49	86

[a]Includes only cases where one spouse receives custody of all the children.

Sex of Parent and Custody Recommendations

In court proceedings, the majority of mothers obtain custody of their children. National Canadian statistics show that in the years 1969 to 1979, 86 percent of mothers as compared to 14 percent of fathers obtained custody when a court decision awarding sole custody of all children to one parent was made. In Ontario, sole custody awards were made in 84 percent of all cases. Split custody (awarding some of the children to each of the parents) was made in 2 percent of the cases. In 12 percent of cases, no award was made. Under the Divorce Act, the judge is not obliged to make a custody order and may choose for various reasons (for example, to respect a previously made custody order) not to issue one. In the remaining 2 percent of the cases, either a custody order that affected only some of the children mentioned in the court action or a custody award to a third party (such as other relatives or a child welfare agency) was made.

The distribution of kinds of custody arrangements recommended by the Custody Project clinicians are quite different from these statistics with the exception of recommendations for sole custody (table 5–12). Perhaps the most interesting difference lies in the lack of preference for mothers over fathers as custodial parents shown by the Custody Project clinicians. Both were equally likely to be seen as the preferred custodial parent.

Children's Age and Sex and Custody Recommendations

A chi-square analysis of the distribution of sole custody recommendations by age and sex of the child showed that mothers and fathers were equally likely to be recommended as custodial parents for children of both sexes at all age levels (table 5–13).

Table 5–13
Sole Custody Recommendations, by Age and Sex of Children

	Age		
	0–5	*6–10*	*11–15*
Boys			
Mother	71%	51%	42%
Father	29	49	58
Girls			
Mother	41	66	61
Father	59	34	39

For the purpose of data collection reasons for making specific custody recommendations were conceptualized in terms of seven major categories:

1. Psychological bonding between parent and child.
2. Continuity of care, which refers here to the maintenance of stability in the child's interpersonal relationships and environment.
3. Children's wishes.
4. Attempt to unite siblings.
5. Parenting ability, which was evaluated in terms of the presence of psychiatric problems, parenting style, time constraints, availability of housing and child care arrangements, and other concerns.
6. Stepparent issues.
7. "Others," which includes considerations such as a child's special physical or emotional needs, the parent's attitude toward the other parent, and the parent's ability to permit contact between the child and the other parent.

Table 5–14 shows the frequency with which these factors influenced the custody recommendations made for boys and girls in each of the three age groups: preschool age, latency age, and preadolescents and adolescents.

Psychological bonding was the reason most frequently mentioned as having influenced the custody recommendation made. It was an influential factor in recommendations made for 72 percent of all children. Although there are some differences among the six subgroups of children in the freqency with which psychological bonding was considered an influential factor (subgroups formed on the basis of age), these differences are not statistically significant.

Children's wishes were the second most frequently stated reason for having made a specific custody recommendation. The custody recommendations made for 65 percent of the children had been strongly influenced by these

Table 5–14
Reasons for Custody Recommendations, by Age Group

	Boys			Girls			Mean
	0–5	6–10	11–15	0–5	6–10	11–15	Percentage
Bonding	79%	55%	61%	80%	81%	74%	72%
Unite siblings	21	21	35	27	33	37	29
Child's wish	58	67	74	47	70	79	65
Continuity of care	84	67	43	87	30	47	59
Mother less fit	18	20	21	16	15	14	17
Father less fit	18	25	31	26	39	33	28
Stepparent issue	10	2	9	0	11	10	7
Other	16	19	22	33	22	0	18
(N)	(19)	(42)	(23)	(15)	(27)	(19)	

children's wishes. With the exception of the youngest subgroup of girls (girls under the age of six), the majority of custody recommendations had been consistent with and influenced by the children's wishes. A statistical analysis showed that older girl's wishes were significantly more often influencing custody decisions than were younger girl's wishes. No such relationship between age and the effect of children's wishes on the recommendations made was found for boys.

About 60 percent of all custody recommendations were influenced by a concern to preserve continuity of care for the children. For children of both sexes, continuity of care was significantly more often stated as a reason for making a custody recommendation for the younger (under six years of age) than the older children ($p < .05$).

The other categories of reasons for making specific custody recommendations were mentioned as having been influential in a minority of cases.

Children's Age, Sex, and
Preference for Sex of Custodial Parent

In the course of the assessments, the majority of children at all age levels had expressed a preference for one parent over the other.

Preschoolers of both sexes chose their mothers more often than their fathers as their preferred custodial parent (table 5–15). Interestingly, among the preschoolers who did prefer the father, girls were overrepresented in comparison to the boys. Among the latency-age children, boys were equally likely to choose either parent, and girls were significantly more likely to prefer to stay with their mothers. In the oldest age group, boys expressed a preference for their fathers more often than for their mothers. The girls were equally likely to choose either parent. There was no significant difference between

Table 5-15
Children's Age, Sex, and Sex of Preferred Parent

Preferred Parent	Boys						Girls						N
	0–5	6–10	11–15		0–5		6–10	11–15					
Mother	9 (41%)	23 (41%)	11 (30%)		10 (43%)		16 (42%)	13 (48%)					82
Father	2 (9%)	19 (34%)	19 (51%)		5 (22%)		5 (13%)	9 (33%)					59
Will not say	11 (50%)	14 (25%)	7 (19%)		8 (35%)		7 (45%)	5 (19%)					52
N	22	56	37		23		38	27					203

the boys and the girls as to their willingness or ability to express a preference for one or the other parent.

Access Recommendations

Investigations of the adjustment of children following separation or divorce have shown that most children long for and benefit from a relationship with the noncustodial parent (Hetherington, Cox, and Cox 1978; Rosen 1977; Wallerstein and Kelly 1980). Proponents of joint custody over sole custody arrangements argue that parental separation should not always also imply a separation between the child and one of his or her parents (Grief 1979; Nehls and Morgenbesser 1980; Roman and Haddad 1978). Within each type of custody arrangement, provisions can be made for maintaining contact between children and both parents. In sole custody arrangements, the relationship between the child and the other parent is usually determined in a so-called visitation or access arrangement. Clinicians writing about assessments and interventions in custody disputes often pay no or very little attention to the issue of access or visitation rights. If the issue is addressed at all, it usually takes the form of a general statement about the advisability of a continuation of a child's relationship with both parents, accompanied by little or no discussion of how this can be accomplished or what kinds of guidelines should be taken into account when making access recommendations.

In this book, considerations regarding access arrangements are treated as of equal importance to those pertaining to custody recommendations (see chapter 9). For the purpose of data collection, Custody Project clinicians conceptualized access arrangements in terms of four major categories: liberal, meaning frequent contacts scheduled by the family according to their needs at the time; structured, meaning that visits occur at a prearranged time and are of specified duration, such as every other weekend, from Saturday at 9 A.M. to Sunday at 6 P.M.; supervised, meaning visits occurring in the presence of a neutral third party; and denial of access, or no contact between the noncustodial parent and his or her children.

The data analysis showed no signficant relationship between the kind of access arrangement recommended and the age or sex of the children (table 5–16). In very few cases was denial of access recommended. The clinicians recommended most often liberal or structured access.

Parental Characteristics and Length of Legal Dispute: Some Concluding Speculations

Relitigation of court-ordered custody arrangements and length of parental dispute regarding the custody of their children are often seen as indexes of

Table 5–16
Access Recommendations, by Age and Sex and Children

	Liberal	Structured	Supervised	No Access	Other	N
Boys						
0–15	10 (42%)	10 (42%)	3 (12%)	0 (0%)	1 (4%)	24
6–10	18 (36%)	17 (34%)	9 (18%)	5 (10%)	1 (2%)	50
11–15	16 (55%)	8 (28%)	1 (3%)	0 (0%)	4 (14%)	29
Girls						
0–5	10 (45%)	8 (37%)	2 (9%)	2 (9%)	0 (0%)	22
6–10	16 (52%)	11 (35%)	1 (3%)	0 (0%)	3 (10%)	31
11–15	15 (65%)	3 (13%)	2 (9%)	1 (4%)	2 (9%)	23

shortcomings of divorcing parents and of the legal and mental health systems serving them (Ilfeld, Ilfeld, and Alexander 1982; Westman 1971). According to these criteria, the Custody Project families are a problem group since they have been involved in litigation longer than most other divorcing parents. The data presented in this chapter allow another, perhaps more compassionate view of these parents and detail at least some of the context within which parents, children, and mental health professionals strive to plan for the continuation of parent–child relationships following parental separation.

Applying criteria such as likelihood of relitigation of a court order means evaluating the family's functioning from the outside: from the perspective of backlogged courts, lawyers, and mental health professionals who may feel frustrated by these parents. In this chapter, we have looked at these families from the inside—their histories, concerns, and current functioning—and have come to see their lengthy legal battles in a somewhat different light.

In most of these families, at least one parent showed signs of a psychiatric disturbance. Many parents had seen the other partner receive inpatient or outpatient psychiatric treatment, or they had been living with the symptoms of his or her emotional problems. About 50 percent of the parents felt that the former spouse's emotional instability had led to the breakup of the marriage. Further, every other parent also was worried about the ex-spouse's child-rearing methods in addition to concerns about his or her other real or imagined shortcomings. A substantial number of these parents were seeing their children exhibit emotional problems, and it would not be too surprising if they felt that the children's difficulties were related to the other parent's deficiencies. The question then arises whether it is unreasonable for a parent who has these kinds of concerns about the former spouse to feel the need to persist in the custody dispute. Would it be perhaps negligent on the part of the parent to give in to the custody demands of the other parent who may be emotionally disturbed and have less to offer to their children? In other words, some parents may have to resort to relitigation because courts, counsel, and mental health professionals have not taken their legitimate concerns into account.

The data show that a third of all custody recommendations made by Custody Project clinicians recommend a change in the existing custody arrangements. Virtually all access recommendations (96 pecent of all access recommendations made) involved a change in the visitation schedule in effect at the time of the assessment. If we assume that these recommendations were made with the children's well-being in mind, then the frequency with which clinicians recommended changes in custody and access arrangements can be seen as justifying at least some of these parents' persistence.

Courts, counsel, and mental health professionals all make mistakes. While there may be parents who resort to relitigation for the wrong reasons— to seek vengeance or to hold on to misperceptions of the other spouse in spite of evidence to the contrary—for example, for some parents, relitigation may be the only avenue to rectify poor court orders and/or poor legal and clinical advice. Others may have to use relitigation to deal with changes in circumstances since a previous court order was made. Only by looking at the length of a custody and/or access dispute in the context of the parents' individual functioning and their concerns about each other and their children can the appropriateness and usefulness of relitigation be evaluated.

Limitations of this Study and Directions for Future Research

For the authors of this book, the most frustrating limitation of the data collection was the lack of follow-up data. Although special efforts were made to recontact some of the families and lawyers involved, not enough data could be collected regarding what happened to these families and the recommendations made following the assessment. At the time of the conclusion of the individual Custody Project assessments, close to 50 percent of the families accepted the recommendations that were made and arrived at a settlement without further litigation. Another third of the families did not agree with the recommendations made, but it is not known whether these recommendations were later incorporated into a court order or whether in time a settlement was reached. In the remaining one-fifth of the cases, no information regarding ultimate acceptance or rejection of the recommendations made was available.

Collecting follow-up data is a time-consuming and expensive process, which went beyond the means of the present study. But it appears that the collection of longitudinal data would be the most appropriate way of studying the fate of these families and whether the clinical interventions and recommendations made had been helpful to them.

Another limitation of this study is the lack of standardized measures of the parents' and children's functioning at the time of the referral and of assessments of changes in them that may have occurred as a result of their involvement in the clinical assessment.

It is usually difficult to reconcile the delivery of clinical services with the requirements of research design; however, the collection of data regarding families who require clinical services for the resolution of custody and/or access disputes and regarding methods of working with them is vital if rational planning of effective clinical services for these families is to occur.

6
The Process of Clinical Intervention

Eric Hood

R eferral to a mental health resource of a child and family because of an emotional or behavioral disorder is expected to result in relief of the child's symptoms and the family's distress. Referral with regard to a custody or access dispute is also expected to address the questions and concerns of the referring lawyers and the court.

MacDonald in chapter 2 described a gradual evolution of judicial attitudes and principles with regard to custody determination, outlining areas that are considered important. A mental health professional is expected to be able to understand and explain these with more facility and objectivity than might a layperson. These areas include stability of home life, continuity of care of children, the capacities of parents to provide physical and emotional care, the needs of the individual child, the strength and quality of emotional ties between parents and children and siblings, the advantages and disadvantages of children's being together or apart, and the preferences and wishes children express about their living arrangements. It is also expected that these areas will be examined and considered in relation to the principle of determining what is in the best interest of each child or is the least detrimental alternative for each child.

Recent legislative changes in various jurisdictions reflect attempts to guide courts in their determination of custody and access. Courts are increasingly expected to consider factors relevant to children's psychological development and to differentiate them clearly from the causes of marital breakdown, so that the children's lives are planned according to their needs rather than according to their parents' marital disabilities.

Responsibilities of the Clinician

The clinician's obligation to the children is to evaluate development, emotional adjustment, relationships, and attachments and to attend to their wishes and concerns, demonstrating that children can contribute to decision making but not control it.

To the parents, the clinician has the obligation of listening objectively and empathically to their concerns, anxieties, wishes, and plans. Clinical intervention should be seen as an opportunity to provide a neutral but concerned milieu in which the parents may be helped to redirect their energies from unproductive, interpersonal struggles toward cooperative planning, in part through reeducation with regard to their children's developmental needs during a period of crisis. This requires an alliance with those aspects of the parents' personalities that express and demonstrate the wish to provide good parenting.

To the referring source, counsel or court, the clinician must be able to provide, from a psychological and developmental point of view, an understanding of the family system and its members, the course of the family breakdown, the children's views of their situation, and the parents' capabilities to develop a new system for the physical and emotional nurturance of the children. From this basis, the clinician is able to discuss the advantages and drawbacks of the custody and access alternatives and to offer recommendations.

In its earliest days, the Custody Project members expected to be able to assess families and to provide the courts with confident recommendations with regard to custody decisions. It soon became apparent, however, that skills in diagnosing individual disorders or patterns of family dysfunction did not always lead to clear-cut conclusions. Often the personality difficulties and emotional disorders that could be identified in parents were not serious enough to rule out consideration of the parent as a full-time caretaker. It was observed that children could remain securely attached and well functioning even if a custodial parent might have a diagnosable mental illness that did not seriously involve the child. In many cases, it was evident that children valued equally the attachments to each parent, both of whom could provide satisfactory, if somewhat different, family environments. A large number of the Custody Project parents could not be described as good or bad; it was necessary to regard each parent as a person of importance to the children and as a person who wished to retain a significant share of the rights and responsibilities of parenthood. Experience showed that decision making by a clinician's opinion had no greater chance of preventing further parental conflict or relitigation than did an imposed court order.

In the early years of the project, it was presumed that the hostility between the parents precluded working jointly with them, but gradually project members began to expect that parents would have some capacity to negotiate with each other and that the project members' obligation to the children compelled them to expect that the parents would try to collaborate in parenting. Thus the education of parents in negotiating with one another became an integral part of the clinical evaluation of the family and its members. This was encouraged by lawyers who perceived the adversarial process as less effective than mediation in settling custody and access disputes.

Litigant Families: The Emotional Context

Families with custody and access diputes have obviously developed a pattern of persistent failure in the resolution of conflicts. Feelings run high, and the climate is filled with intense emotions. Anxiety, anger, guilt, and sadness are all observable. Often the war has been long and exhausting; almost half of the Custody Project families had been in litigation for more than a year, a third for up to three years, and almost a fifth for more than three years prior to referral.

The prospect of face-to-face meetings in the clinician's office raises anxiety. Parents often worry about controlling anger and express fear of violent behavior. More than half of the couples following separation had continuing disagreements with regard to child-rearing practices. Financial and property disputes, intrusive behavior, and denigration of the former spouse and the new marital partner to the children were also complained about frequently.

Much of the behavioral and emotional conflict between separated parents can be understood as a reflection of their inability to mourn successfully the loss of their idealized marital relationship and of the loss of a significant attachment figure (Weiss 1975). In case presentations, the Custody Project clinicians repeatedly described compulsive, litigious, suspicious parents, more often fathers, who showed intense interest in ex-spouses and who conducted bizarre legal battles. It has been the project members' conclusion that such parents are unable to relinquish the fantasy of a compliant and pleasing partner since this would result in a narcissistic injury.

Working with such a population can be exhausting. Clinicians are understandably reluctant to expose themselves to the stresses encountered in such difficult family systems. Into this painful atmosphere, the clinician must be able to bring optimism and a sense of personal security. The family members must be provided with a sense of structure and security at all times. The clinician must be firm in developing and upholding rules regarding behavior within the sessions. It must be made clear that impulsive behavior or hostile verbal attacks will not be permitted and that in individual sessions there is little value in persistent denigration of the other parent.

Assessment Process

Despite the parental separation, the family continues to be a complex system of relationships, with continuing conflict and distress. A family systems approach is advocated with the aim of bringing conflicting forces together into a working alliance with the clinician in the interests of the children (Group for the Advancement of Psychiatry 1980).

Contracting

While the basic contract in the Custody Project is negotiated between clinician and lawyers on behalf of their clients, it must be recapitulated in greater detail with the family members. At the point of assignment of the case to a clinician, parents know that they will be seen together, individually, and in various combinations with their children. The parents usually respect the clinician's position of neutrality but often have questions about the number of interviews or the length of the assessment process.

In the initial interviews, whether individual, with both parents, or with the whole family, the clinician attempts to establish that the focus of the assessment will be the developmental needs of the children and the importance of both parents to them. The parents' agreement is obtained for any information from or involvement with other parties, such as extended family members, babysitters, day care staff, teachers, and family physicians. Written consents for the release of information are signed. If at this point a parent has major reservations about the clinician's procedures or refuses permission for contact with a significant source of information, the parent is asked to discuss those concerns with counsel. No further clinical activity is undertaken unless the parent is able to overcome his or her anxieties and permit the clinician to gather the information deemed necessary.

Clinical Procedures

Although each clinician in the project has worked independently, in general the procedures have been carried out in approximately the following sequence:

1. Counsel are contacted by telephone or in a joint interview in order to reinforce the professional alliance and to clarify particular issues in the case.

2. The initial contracting interview(s) with parents and children focuses on the assessment's purposes and procedures. Individual and joint interviews are then arranged. In some instances, this initial contracting has been done in an interview with the parents only. Occasionally, on the basis of counsels' experience with their clients, the contracting is done individually with each parent, particularly if there is extreme fearfulness about face-to-face contact.

3. Parents are interviewed individually, each usually requiring two sessions.

4. Each child is interviewed individually.

5. The children are seen together.

6. Interviews are carried out with extended family members, including new partners, stepsiblings, and grandparents or others who are closely involved with the children's lives.

7. Psychological testing is obtained if requested by the clinician.

8. The children are observed and interviewed with parents or with other significant adults, sometimes at home.

9. Information is integrated from written reports or telephone calls from schools, agencies, day care staff, physicians, and previously involved mental health personnel.

10. Parents are given jointly the clinician's findings for discussion and negotiation-mediation.

11. The case is presented for consultation in a Custody Project meeting.

12. The clinician's findings and the outcome of the assessment-mediation process are given to counsel, often in a face-to-face meeting and always in a written report.

13. Custody and access recommendations are given to parents if no agreement between them has been possible. This is more likely to be done in individual interviews because the parents are highly polarized and see themselves in terms of winning or losing the case.

It can be seen that a considerable number of hours will be used with this approach and that the assessment process may take many weeks (tables 6–1 and 6–2). Two-thirds of the cases took more than two months to complete, and some continued for much longer. The majority of cases requiring more hours over more weeks were those in which access was the primary dispute. Mediation of these often involved a period of time in which access was supervised by the clinician. While it is desirable to avoid having families endure

Table 6–1
Clinician Hours Required

Number of Hours	Percentage of Families
2–4	5
5–9	32
10–12	30
13–18	23
19–25	10

Table 6–2
Length of Time to Case Completion

Number of Weeks	Percentage of Cases
1–2	10
3–6	30
7–9	25
10–20	26
21 or more	8

prolonged anxiety about the outcome of assessments and while efforts to provide rapid intense assessments by a clinical team have much to commend them, it can also be argued that the process of change must often be slow and that highly polarized parents require time for reflection and debate before being able to relinquish the fantasies of their preferred solutions (Benedek and Benedek 1972; Goldstein, Freud, and Solnit 1973; Jackson et al. 1980).

Interviews

Sequencing of Interviews

Early in the project's history, most initial interviews were conducted separately with each parent. It was increasingly felt within the project's discussions, however, that the initial contracting interviews should be carried out with at least both parents and preferably with the total family present. Such interviews can be extremely anxiety laden for all of the participants and require firm control by the clinician. Some of the project clinicians see the initial family interview as essential and are reluctant to carry out the assessment without it, while others are prepared to accede to parents' anxieties and begin with individual or conjoint interviews, working toward family interviews when they judge them to be more tolerable.

Clinicians who advocate family interviews in the beginning wish to emphasize the family system focus and to demonstrate to the parents that their major concerns are the needs of the children rather than the competing interests of the parents. Early inclusion of the children enables the clinician to elicit their thoughts and feelings and to ensure that these are heard and understood by the parents. Having the parents leave the first family interview after the initial contracting has been carried out allows the clinician and children to relax with each other, and the children can become familiar with the clinician and the setting. Another advantage of an initial family interview is that it ensures that all members of the family are involved together in the contracting and that the parents see that they are being treated equally and without bias by the clinician.

Interviews with Parents

In individual interviews, each parent can provide personal and family history, an account of the marital relationship, and the developmental histories of the children. The clinician collects sufficient information to be able to evaluate the emotional state of each parent and to determine whether there is any disturbance present. In addition, particular attention is paid to the parents' family histories and the parenting that they received, including any disruptions in relationships with their parents. The parents' developmental histories can reveal the presence of neurotic or characterological patterns that might interfere with productivity, reliability, consistency, or the ability to sustain adequate relationships with partners or children. History of psychiatric treatment may indicate not only previous disability but, more positively, also attempts at problem solving and personal growth.

Irrespective of the findings of psychiatric illness or personality disorder in parents, it has nonetheless been the hope of the project's clinicians to form an alliance with those aspects of the parents that are well functioning. Psychiatric disturbance in itself need not lead to poor parenting. It is important to assess the parents' capacity to distinguish their own needs and wishes from those of the children. Considerable time must be spent in discussion of the parents' plans for the children's living arrangements and the changes that may be needed as children become older. Each parent's capacity to tolerate and understand the importance of the children's relationship with the other parent must be assessed.

Review of the marital history can help a parent to recall the strengths or attractions once seen in the other partner, and it may be possible to reshape distorted views of the ex-spouse, at least with regard to parenting ability.

Parents list many problems leading to the marital breakdown. These are stated with great conviction, although the clinician may find that the same events and processes are described differently by each parent. Custody Project clinicians repeatedly found themselves torn by the apparent plausibility of both partners. The consequent stress that the clinicians experienced probably resembles the loyalty conflict suffered by the children in these disrupted families. Considerable effort is required to help the parents refocus from these bitter complaints toward a more cooperative approach in the interests of the children.

Individual Assessment of the Child

As in any other clinical assessment, it is necessary to evaluate the child in comparison with developmental norms. Basic adjustment in family relationships, at school, with peers, and within the community should be reviewed and postseparation changes noted. The quality of attachments to parents, siblings, and other significant figures must be understood, and the capacity to use substitutes for an absent parent has been emphasized (Group for the Advancement of Psychiatry 1980). In the light of the general belief that the children of separated parents suffer considerable distress, the question of psychiatric impairment and the possible need for treatment must be thoroughly considered.

Interviewing techniques may vary considerably but must be appropriate to the child's age and developmental level. Preschoolers and children in the early school years are best assessed in a playroom where doll houses, puppet families, drawing materials, and games are available. Periods of structured and unstructured activity should be used as the clinician evaluates cognitive, motor, verbal, social, and emotional aspects of development.

Some children may require a considerable period of time before painful family issues can be dealt with, but a considerable number are eager to express their thoughts and wishes.

In addition to evaluating the child's psychiatric status, the clinician must also make it clear to the child that his or her task is to help the family resolve its dispute and to understand those difficulties that may produce worry, sadness, and disappointment for the child. A simple explanation about the clinician's familiarity with children's problems usually encourages discussion.

It is useful to ask open-ended questions about children's concerns. These may often be in relation to practical matters such as time spent with parents, missing treats and outings, being unable to see friends regularly, being unable to take toys or clothes back and forth between the parents' homes, exposure to parental quarreling, worry about their parents' emotional adjustment, and feeling responsible for the marital breakdown. Much of this information can gradually be obtained within the context of low-key discussions about daily routines, access visits, differing parenting styles, and the material aspects of life with each parent.

Although it is easier for older children to consider objectively the possible living alternatives, even children in their early school years can explore these issues in interviews and reveal their concerns and preoccupations. With preschoolers, pictures and doll play provide an opportunity for expression of the child's view of the world and of significant relationships. Children can be encouraged to express their fantasies regarding custody or access changes. With younger children the most frequently expressed wish is to have both parents available. When new partners are involved, the children often readily include them in the reunion fantasy, demonstrating their wish for involvement with all concerned and affectionate adults.

Johnny, age nine, was brought for consultation by his father and step-mother. During a summer visit, he had stated that he wished to remain with them, although he had been in his mother's care, in another province, for four years since the separation, with only occasional contact with his father. Johnny's father was torn between sticking to the established agreement and taking action to change custody. During interviews, it became clear that Johnny had a happy life with his mother, but his summer visit had given him such pleasure that he was reluctant to let it end. Johnny's positive feelings about his mother were clearly expressed in a joint interview with his father and stepmother, who were startled to hear him state that he would like to have all three parent figures living together with him. Johnny's father was thus able to become more aware of his son's view of family relationships and attempted to maintain closer contact, relinquishing the idea of a custody change at that time.

As children discuss the alternative plans put forward by parents, they may be able to offer other solutions that the adults have not considered. It is usually believed that children's attachments to the family home, the neighborhood, schools, and friends are extremely significant and should be disrupted as little as possible; however, children do not always see these as of overriding importance.

Initially Custody Project clinicians felt concerned about burdening children by asking them to state preferences with regard to custody; however, most authors think that the question must be put in some way. Some ask it early and discuss it actively in individual and joint sessions (Levy 1978; Kargman 1979). Of the Custody Project's 215 children, 70 percent are reported to have expressed a preference, and of these somewhat more than half (58 percent) of the children stated a preference for living with their mother. Preferences were rated for strength. Most had been strongly stated. It appeared that only about one-third of the parents had actively encouraged the children to state their own wishes to the clinician.

Assessment of the Sibling Group

In all families, the sibling group is a potent and significant subsystem. With the breakdown of the marriage, the children may take on increased responsibility for maintenance of the emotional and instrumental supports within the family. While some children may be more at ease expressing preferences to clinicians when seen alone, for others it is more comfortable to discuss alternative plans among the siblings (Chasin and Grunebaum 1981). The interviews with the sibling group can also be used to encourage the children to discuss their concerns and preferences with the parents.

Observation of the sibling group in the office or the playroom also reveals roles and functions that children may take. For example, an older child may function as a substitute parent. Particular attachments or difficulties between children may be observed and can be helpful in determining the most appropriate living arrangements for them.

Generally there is a presumption that siblings should not be separated; however, it can be argued that in some cases, there are valid emotional or practical reasons for dividing the children. Children's ideas about this should be explored, and it will often be found that they have considered being split and that they even have a plan to offer. Only 10 percent of children with siblings in the Custody Project sample stated a wish to keep the sibling group intact regardless of which parent obtained custody.

> *Eleven-year-old Jane had stated to her parents that she wished to leave her mother's new home and live with her father, near the old family home. Both parents had new partners. "It's not that I don't love my Mum, but I've always been closer to my Dad," she said. Nine-year-old Sharon, obviously very attached to Jane, agreed and added, "I'm closer to my Mum." The girls had discussed how to maintain contact on weekends and were eager to have their parents agree to the plan and stop quarreling.*

Joint Parent–Child Interviews

Depending on the ages and circumstances of children, joint parent–child interviews can include discussions in the office, playroom activity, home visits, and outdoor sessions (for example, in a garden or park). Parents are understandably anxious about being observed in interaction with their children. The clinician can put them at ease by encouraging them to take charge of the children, particularly in unstructured or play situations. Ideally there should be an opportunity for the clinician to involve parents and children in joint discussion of the family's custody and living arrangements, with thorough consideration of the alternatives. Parents should also have an opportunity to discuss less contentious issues with the children, such as day-to-day family functioning, the children's behavior, school performance, and sibling relationships, so that they can be seen as functioning parents and not only as litigants.

Observation of parents and children in the playroom can provide considerable information, but the rather artificial situation can be threatening to an anxious parent. The clinician can put the parent at ease by being close at hand and readily discussing issues such as child development and behavior. This keeps the interview child focused while adding to the clinician's knowledge about the parent's understanding and expectations of children.

Other Interviews

Interviews that include other persons such as new spouses, stepsiblings, and extended family members may be necessary, depending on their significance to the lives of the children. The project's clinicians have routinely seen new spouses, common-law partners, and stepsiblings who are part of the day-to-day family system in either living situation. Babysitters and others who carry major child-rearing responsibility need to be evaluated and can provide another source of information.

Psychological Testing

The project did not carry out routine psychological testing. The clinicians tended to reserve its use for cases in which there was diagnostic uncertainty. The presence or extent of psychopathology, the level of intellectual functioning, the presence of paranoid thinking, and personality characteristics were areas in which clinicians most often asked for confirmation or clarification by testing of parents. With regard to children, clinicians usually asked about comparisons with developmental and intellectual norms and differences in attitude toward males and females.

The use of testing may also confirm the presence of maladaptive personality characteristics in a parent who is highly resistant to the clinician's efforts at problem solving and mediation. It is thus possible to use the test results as a second opinion, illustrating to counsel that the clinician's recommendations are not the result of bias or personality conflict.

> *Mr. Brown, a successful businessman who remained unyielding during efforts to compromise about the sharing of child-rearing responsibilities and rights, complained to his lawyer that the male clinician had been personally prejudiced against him and had sided with his wife. Psychological tests confirmed the clinician's impression of Mr. Brown's rigidity, egocentricity, and omnipotence. Their objectivity reassured the lawyer in regard to the question of bias.*

Written Documents

In addition to the numerous interviews, the clinician also makes use of documents submitted to the court and reports from schools, day care programs, physicians, mental health professionals, child protection agencies, and other community resources with whom the family has had extensive contact. In order to comprehend fully the background of a legal battle, it is important to review documents such as affidavits and judgments that are part of the legal case record. In cases where violence or antisocial behavior is alleged, it is appropriate to request that the parents sign releases to obtain police records.

Formulation and Case Presentation

Having gathered a considerable amount of information, the clinician formulates the case, developing hypotheses about the evolution of the family system and the individual members, paying attention to their strengths and weaknesses, as well as their disturbances or developmental lags. Each parent must be considered in relation to:

1. Mental health functioning and personality style as it relates to parenting capacity (Group for the Advancement of Psychiatry 1980).
2. Capacity to provide physical and emotional care within a continuous and stable environment.
3. Capacity to understand objectively the developmental needs of each of the children.
4. Ability to differentiate between personal wishes and the children's needs and to relate to the child as an individual rather than as an extension of the self.
5. Capacity to understand, tolerate, and support the child's attachment to the other parent.
6. Capacity to develop flexibility in negotiating with the other parent.

The formulation process should consider the mental health status of each child and the temperamental or personality style, particularly as it applies to parent–child and sibling attachments. The clinician must speculate about the varying developmental needs of children at different ages, bearing in mind such factors as the need for early adolescents to identify closely with the same-sex parents, the difficulty for early latency children in tolerating family breakup, the expressed wishes for frequent contact with the absent parent, and the need for frequent but brief contacts between preschoolers and the noncustodial parent so that established relationships can be maintained without disrupting the stability and consistency of daily routines.

At this point it has been common for the case to be presented and discussed in a project meeting. Custody Project members have been particularly helpful to each other in identifying difficult countertransference reactions, usually toward a parent. In work with disputing parents, it is likely that the more flexible parent will be more likable; therefore clinicians must be observant of their own reactions to the parents. Group discussions have also helped to extend the efforts of the clinicians—for example, in the areas of mediation between the parents or in working with lawyers. Project clinicians have stated frequently that they would be unwilling to be involved in such complicated cases if it were not for the availability of a support group.

Mediation Stage

Efforts at mediation intensify following evaluation of all the parties within the family system, although it is artificial to suggest that it is a separate stage since the clinician will have made some effort at mediation in even the earliest interviews. For example, difficulties around current access arrangements can provide an opportunity for the parents to demonstrate their readiness to make use of a neutral mediator.

During mediation efforts, it should be made clear to the parents that the clinician's concern is with the sharing of responsibilities rather than with the winning or losing of custody. In the case of the parental dyads that appear prepared to negotiate, the clinician can begin by reviewing the findings with regard to each of the children and the positive aspects of the relationships between parents and children.

Discussion of the strengths and drawbacks of each plan should be undertaken, and, as in therapy, the clinician should be prepared to use a number of sessions to help the parents to consider thoroughly all options. Parents may wish to consult counsel, and counsel should be aware of the clinician's efforts during this period.

In more acrimonious cases, it may be preferable to recruit the professional authority of the parents' counsel and present the findings to them, giving particular emphasis to the strengths and weaknesses of any of the plans that have been advocated by parents, children, or clinician. Counsel may then proceed to negotiate with their clients to reach resolution, perhaps with involvement of the clinician, and without resorting to a court hearing.

Presentation of Findings and Recommendations

In clinical work, it is usually expected that findings will be presented in one or more interviews. It has been suggested that when a parent can be perceived as the loser, he or she should be seen first, and particular help should be given to facilitate the grieving process (Warner and Elliott 1979).

In the Custody Project cases, such interviews are followed by a written report to counsel and to the court, if the referral has been requested by a judge. As the project clinicians became more experienced in working with counsel, there were increasing efforts to involve them during the assessment and prior to the preparation of the written report. Presentation of the clinician's opinion about the various custody and access options enables counsel to take responsibility in the mediation process and to work collaboratively with the clinician in attempting to gain the parents' commitment to a plan. At times it may even be unnecessary for the clinician to make specific, detailed recommendations since the findings about the needs of the children and the capacities of the parents may indicate the probable outcome should the case return to court. If custody is settled, the parents can shift their attention to arranging access.

Postassessment Process

In just over half of the cases seen in the Custody Project, the clients were unable to reach agreement, and the case returned to court. In such cases, the clinician's written report acquired great significance when submitted to court. At times the clinicians were required to attend court for cross-examination in regard to their work. Most court hearings, however, did not require the attendance of the clinician; the report itself was sufficient.

Written Report

While no two clinicians report in exactly the same format, the following outline is generally regarded as appropriate for the purposes of the Court. A sample report is contained in appendix B.

Statement of Qualifications

A brief paragraph should describe the clinician's qualifications and training so that the report can be validly accepted as evidence by the court.

Referral Information

A brief statement is made about the clinician's understanding of the purpose of the referral and the questions being asked by counsel or the court.

Summary of Assessment Activity

A list of interviews, testing sessions, and visits should include dates and the names of participants.

Individual History of Parents

This section should provide a summary of each parent's background as a basis for understanding subsequent information and observations about the parent's capacity to take care of the children. As much as possible, the report should protect each parent's confidentiality. This section should include each parent's current situation and the alternatives proposed for child care and access.

Marital History According to Each Parent

This information may be given in more or less detail, but it is important to show an awareness of the differing perceptions of each partner and to explain those differences in accordance with an understanding of each parent. Some authors modify reports so that not all parental information goes out to all parties (Lewis 1974; Solow and Adams 1977). Since a report submitted to court will become a matter of public record, the Custody Project participants feel obliged to provide reports that can be read by any of the litigants and their counsel and to write them carefully using language that will be as inoffensive as possible.

Developmental History of Each Child

This section should summarize the parents' descriptions of the children. Conflicting opinions between the parents should be noted.

Interviewing Impressions

A summary should be provided of the clinician's interviewing impressions of each person seen and of the various joint interviews that have been carried out. This section should demonstrate to the lawyers or court the extent and the thoroughness of the assessment.

Other Material

Summaries of psychological test results and reports from other professionals or agencies should be referred to in order to indicate the sources of information used in the assessment.

Discussion and Recommendations

This section should include a clinical formulation in easy-to-understand language. It should demonstrate how the clinician has used information and observations to develop an understanding of the family and its difficulties. It should also include consideration of the plans or proposals advocated by the parents and of any others that have been introduced by the clinician. Discussion of the advantages and drawbacks of all options should be stated, noting those with which one or other parent disagrees.

Any recommendations for subsequent treatment of one or more family members should be included in the report. If the parents and clinician agree that it would be useful for the clinician to provide a milieu for supervised access, this should be offered as a part of the settlement.

Summary

Intervention in custody and access disputes must be undertaken with an awareness of the clinician's responsibilities to counsel and court, as well as to children and parents. It is important to assess and to understand the complexities of the disrupted family system and not simply to compare the parents as rival caretakers. Family assessment and attempts at mediation require numerous appointments, including conjoint and family sessions, which may be tense and stressful. Firm control is needed from the clinician, with the support of counsel.

Assessment should include stepparents, stepsiblings, and others who are closely involved with the children, who should be seen in interaction with them, as well as with parents.

The clinician should presume that compromise and mediation will be preferable to litigation and that the parents share this attitude. In order to mediate between the parents, it is essential to have developed a thorough understanding of the individual family members and the system of family relationships by history taking and clinical observations.

Children usually have preferences about custody and access arrangements and are often relieved to be able to express them to an interested outsider. They should be encouraged to explore the advantages and drawbacks of the various proposals. Thus they develop increased mastery of their situation.

The clinician must assess a number of aspects of parenting style and not only the mental health status of parents.

Presentation of these difficult cases to colleagues provides support and encouragement, which is essential for the prevention of clinician burn-out. Presentation of clinical findings in meetings with lawyers may facilitate compromise and mediation. Written reports should demonstrate the thoroughness of the clinical work and should be written in simple language that parents and counsel can easily understand. Well-written reports can reduce the frequency of attendance at court and shorten the amount of time needed for examination or cross-examination.

7
Therapeutic Considerations: Techniques of Intervention

Elsa A. Broder

C risis is defined as an "upset in a steady state" where "habitual problem-solving activities are not adequate and do not lead rapidly to the previously achieved balanced state" (Rapoport 1962, p. 24). The words *crisis* and *stress* are often used interchangeably, with usually negative connotation, implying disaster, calamity, tension, or pain. But *crisis* also can have the more positive meaning of "turning point" or "climax." As such, it can catalyze change in the ways members of the family relate to one another, disrupting old habits and evoking new responses. Some families, however, cannot respond to the challenge and may turn to mental health professionals for help. Therapeutic intervention at this time can provide one of the few opportunities in the field of mental health for primary intervention.

This chapter will consider some of the literature on family systems as it pertains to separation and divorce and the ways the clinician can work with the family at that time. The goals of intervention, characteristic problems, and ways of working with families after the custody and access dispute is settled will also be discussed.

Theoretical Considerations

In the beginning two people meet, fall in love, and decide they want to make a commitment to live together and share in the responsibility of raising their children. Each family develops its own idiosyncratic structure and ways of performing daily tasks and making decisions. Mechanisms operating at both intrapsychic and interpersonal levels must be in place to maintain equilibrium (homeostatis) and to allow the family to respond to change. For all families "change is, in fact, the norm, and a long range view of family would show great flexibility, constant fluctuation, and quite probably more disequilibrium than balance" (Minuchin and Fishman 1981, p. 21). If the family does not have adequate means of accommodating to change, stress increases and may result in symptomatology in one of the family members or family breakup (Hoffman 1981; Minuchin and Fishman 1981; Mandanes 1981).

By definition, separation means change in the family configuration. Roles must be reassigned and new ways evolved of transacting with one another. Husband and wife lose a partner; the children, at least on a day-to-day basis, lose a parent. Both parents may be less available emotionally and physically. Economically the family is usually poorer, often necessitating that both parents work (Luepnitz 1982; Spanier and Casto 1979; Bloom, White, and Asher 1979; Hetherington, Cox, and Cox 1976). There may not be sufficient extra money for entertainment or other recreational activities.

Behavior in separation and divorce, as in all other crises, appears to be "determined by the interaction of at least four factors including a) influences of the situation itself, b) the pre-existing personality, c) the cultural factors and d) interaction with significant others" (Caplan, Mason, and Kaplan, 1973, p. 130).

Anxiety and depression are frequent sequelae (Weiss 1975; Bloom, White, and Asher 1979). Old, partly unresolved, unconscious conflicts may be reactivated (Thomas 1982). The children show their distress in ways congruent with their stage of development and understanding of what is happening (Wallerstein and Kelly 1980; Rutter 1971). Many shy away from contact with others, feeling that they will be a burden or that others will not understand or take sides. Sound advice and information may be disregarded even though it is desperately needed for the family to reorganize to reach a new homeostasis or balance.

Both parties may not be equally committed to the separation. One or both may use litigation as a way of clarifying feelings about the past relationship, as a means of maintaining the status quo, avoiding a real separation, or as a means of retaliation (Goode 1956; Brown 1976; Johnston, Campbell, and Tall 1985; Weiss 1975). The persistence of attachment, distress over the failed relationship, and ambivalence about wanting the divorce mitigate against the resolution of conflict.

Relatives and friends come forth with a plethora of suggestions, usually contradictory in nature. Previously mutual family friends become "his" or "hers." Although separation and divorce are no longer unusual phenomena, the stigma remains, even for the children, and the social-cultural context is disrupted.

> It was parent–teacher night at Alice Gerrard's school. She wanted to go and visit her friends while her parents talked with the teacher and inspected her work. Mr. and Mrs. Gerrard were not willing to attend together and could not come to an agreement as to who should go. Alice felt ashamed and did not know how to explain her own absence to her friends because she had kept her parents' separation and imminent divorce secret.

In the crisis of separation, time is of the essence in helping families to avoid becoming stuck in chronic, repetitive, conflictual ways of relating to one another. The opportunity is there to resolve impasses and to help the process of uncoupling. Nevertheless, it is important that the clinician not misinterpret the severity of the situation or the behavior and regard all separated individuals and families as patients. To do so would rob the individuals involved of the opportunity to benefit from their troubles and to grow in ways that could not have been predicted.

Within the field of family therapy, there are several views as to how change is achieved (Feldman 1976). Some believe that through insight, people are able to change how they feel and behave. Others downgrade insight and emphasize instead techniques of operant and classical conditioning, modeling, and cognitive restructuring. Still others consider paradox to be the most potent agent of change. Insight is important in the sense that parents may need education about normal reactions to their situation, interpretation of the behaviors that they and the children may be demonstrating and how their behaviors relate to unresolved conflict from the past. The parents must learn that what has happened before is not always a good indicator of what can happen in the future and that an unsatisfactory spouse can still be a supportive and reliable coparent (Wallerstein and Kelly 1980).

Lack of ability in problem solving and conflict resolution were probably important factors in the breakup of the marriage (Kessler 1975). Hence, teaching of communication and problem-solving skills is an important part of the therapeutic process. Paradoxical techniques are generally not useful or necessary, except possibly with extremely intransigent and chronically litigating couples. Although there is a burgeoning of literature on the use of paradox in therapy, no reports of its use in this context were found. To help families resolve conflict, the clinician must couple a model of how change can occur with knowledge of normal individual development, family life cycles and tasks, and the range of reactions that people can have to separation.

Therapeutic Alliance

The achievement of a therapeutic alliance is important but hard to achieve. Because the family has been through difficult, disillusioning, and conflictual times, the ability to trust may be low. The usual expectation that a clinician will be helpful, which in itself may produce amelioration of symptoms (the so-called waiting list cure or the placebo effect), may not be present. Often the clinician is seen as the enemy and an obstacle to be circumvented or as a needed advocate to be won over. The reaction to the clinician may be a manifestation of transference reactions or a reflection of what they have been told or have understood about the process.

The children too may resist forming an alliance with the clinician. They may be terrified that they will be asked to reveal unsavory facts about one or both parents or to choose which parent they would prefer to live with, creating intolerable loyalty conflicts.

Yet work cannot proceed without some trust and respect. The client must learn that the clinician will listen empathically but will not be manipulated, take sides, or allow aggression of either a psychological or physical nature to occur. A constructive, controlled atmosphere must be achieved to set the tone for future negotiations. Taking charge, maintaining a neutral stance, preventing extreme emotionality and badgering, keeping the process goal directed, and focusing on the needs of the children are helpful techniques in achieving the goal of a therapeutic alliance.

Reactions of the Clinician

Expectations of the clinicians are very high and unrelenting by both the family and the legal system. When the family is in obvious pain, it is hard to know what to do first: attempt to relieve the pain or get on with the assignment. The clinician must act as judge, mediator, educator, supporter, corrector of mind set and prejudices, guide to behavior, and last, therapist, depending on how the family members are feeling and where they are in the process of uncoupling. To know which role to pursue for how long is a vexing problem.

It is not only the variety of roles the clinicians must play that makes this work difficult. The reactions of the clinician may be the product of confusion over roles, reaction to the adversary system based on ideological differences or ignorance of the norms and rules of behavior, hearing things that go against one's sensibilities, if not morality, overidentification with the children, reaction against being expected to have King Solomon's wisdom, and countertransference reactions. Some of the individuals involved are not particularly likable, and their behavior can be despicable. The children are pathetic, and it is extremely difficult not to be angry at the parents for using them as a battleground. Intense anger and hostility between the spouses is often present. Threats of violence may be directed not only at the partner but at the clinician as well.

> *Mr. Kyle had been diagnosed as suffering from a paranoid state and had a history of assaulting with a knife some females who thwarted him. The clinician's final recommendation was that the custody of the children be transferred from him to his former wife. For months after, the clinician found herself feeling apprehensive when she had to go alone to the parking lot at night and was concerned that the father might repeat his previous behavior.*

More than any other work that clinicians do, it is impossible to escape the realization that in a profound way what is done and what is decided will have a major impact on the lives of all involved. Therefore it is of the utmost importance that the clinician have a colleague or a consultation group with whom reactions and judgments can be discussed to ensure that objectivity is not clouded and that all alternatives are considered.

Assessment Meetings

At the time the assessment process begins, the spouses may not have seen each other face to face for months or even years and may have developed exaggerated notions about the negative characteristics of the other. If the parents are to develop an ability to negotiate issues regarding the needs of the children, each must be able to face the other asserting his or her position. They must learn how to listen to the other's point of view and consider the validity of what is being said before responding. The importance of this face-to-face contact may have to be explained to the lawyers so that they can ensure their client's attendance.

By bringing the whole family together, including the children, the process of demythification can begin, and distortions are avoided. The children can have an opportunity to see their parents together in the same room and to obtain reassurance that their parents will act in concert on their behalf. The family sessions permit information to be shared and misperceptions clarified. Most parents will try to moderate their behavior when the children are present if for no other reason but to impress the clinician. It is not necessary to be excessively concerned about the effect of parental disagreement on the children, providing the clinician is comfortable in using authority to ensure that it does not get out of hand. The children have been exposed to fighting many times over. The clinician attempts to align with the children and the good and caring parts of the parents.

Nevertheless, some parents may be so upset that they are not able to assimilate the information given in the family session. The data that have been shared may have to be repeated to be meaningful. Occasionally feelings are so intense that holding a family meeting is not profitable. Separate meetings can be held with the goal of working through feelings in order to move toward face-to-face contact. The most salient factor usually is the clinician's confidence in seeing the family together. It is not uncommon to hear that after a family interview, the parents talked together constructively for the first time in years.

During assessment, the parents are encouraged to review what has happened and to look at their individual role in the events, with no one being permitted to place all the blame on others. Contrary to what is sometimes advocated in family therapy, history is important (Haley 1977; Minuchin and Fishman 1981; Jordan 1982). The search for repetitive patterns of behavior that led to discord helps to achieve an understanding of how the parents fight and of the obstacles to dispute resolution. This information can be employed to develop new problem-solving strategies.

For a variety of reasons, one or both parents may have become stuck in completing the process of mourning the loss of the marriage. For the healthier, the review of past events coupled with judicious probing and confrontation may help in getting the process of mourning resumed. For others, more extensive therapy may be needed and recommended. Parents may be afraid to seek therapy, feeling that this will influence their chances of gaining custody or access. Explanation of the negative effects of their distress on the children and how therapy is looked upon by the clinician may overcome resistance.

For the children, the interviews may be the first opportunity that they have had to express their wishes, fears, and misunderstandings freely. Opportunity is provided for them to ask questions and reveal feelings long kept secret. Tensions may be eased by sharing the experiences of other children caught in a similar situation (Gardner 1976). The clinician must be sensitive to loyal conflicts and must not create undue stress by pushing too hard to procure the child's preference. Obstacles for the child in sharing feelings with parents must be explored and, where indicated, encouragement given to approach one or both parents about what is being felt or to obtain clarification and support that has not been forthcoming. The normal hierarchy of the family where parents make decisions must be upheld, although the children's views of the situation are important.

Although siblings can be an important support system, children may be afraid to talk with a sibling for fear of ridicule or of placing an undue burden on the sibling or fear that what is said will be reported to the parents. The meeting with the children without the adults can be used to encourage the children to talk with one another and to reach out for support, validation, approval, and even for advocacy. However, not all the children in the family may be in agreement about custody, and isomorphically they may replicate the fights of the parents.

> *When the Smiths separated, they decided that their three children would remain with the mother. The eldest girl and youngest boy were very attached to their mother and resisted visiting their father. The middle child, a girl, enjoyed the visits but experienced difficulty because of the teasing by her siblings when she returned from visiting. Work had to be done with the mother regarding how she was subtly influencing the children, allowing harassment of the middle child.*

Presentation of Findings

After all the necessary information has been obtained, the material must be integrated and formulated so that a strategy for change facilitation is developed. The transmission of the opinion may be the most demanding aspect for the clinician because one or both parents may be disappointed, feeling they have lost. Some recommend giving the findings to the parent who will lose custody first, to prevent their learning about the findings in a destructive way (Warner and Elliott 1979). Others meet both parents or the whole family together so that they can work out the change in organization together. Regardless of which format is chosen, the findings must be presented in such a way that no one's self-esteem is compromised, stressing the positive contribution that each parent can make to the future development and well-being of the children. The behavior that has been seen and the needs of the children must be explained fully, making clear the underlying dynamics and each child's developmental requirements. Education may be necessary for parents to see that the involvement of both is required for the children to grow in a healthy way. The pain of loss of children, family, and even contest must be eased, helping all maintain their sense of integrity. By keeping the focus on the needs of the children in the present and the future, the clinician can facilitate the parent's ability to hear the report.

The clinician should aim to help the parents to accept the findings and to negotiate a plan compatible with the needs of the children and with the family members' way of life. Methods of conflict resolution can be taught to the parents, and rules can be established to facilitate communication, thus attempting to establish new patterns of problem solving.

A major impediment to problem solving is excessive emotionality. Relaxation techniques and the use of time out or thought stoppage are helpful to moderate the intensity of feelings. Some clients may need personal therapy before they are able to relate to the former spouse in a constructive fashion.

Possible reactions on the part of both parents and children should be anticipated with suggestions as to how each parent might change his or her behavior to avoid conflict in the future. Encouragement is given to mutual sharing of information about the children. For example, both parents should see report cards and medical reports. Communication about important happenings on visits may often be managed by telephone. Work may have to be done in this regard because each parent may tend to assume that any difficulties will be seen negatively and used destructively by the other. Children invariably will be naughty, ill, have accidents, be upset, misunderstand events, or be manipulative. Parents must learn how to share information without making premature value judgments, leveling accusations, or feeling threatened.

At times, however, difficult face-to-face contact between the parents will be necessary if they are to share the parenting of their children. Use of a public place, like a restaurant, encourages civil behavior. For some, face-to-face contact may not be possible without a third person present. The couple may need to continue to use the clinician or have a trusted friend or relative present when important decisions must be made. Others find the telephone or writing to produce less tension and to be more efficient. In general, for both efficiency and clarity, direct contact is more desirable than going through a third party.

During the phase when the clinician's findings are given and the parents are expected to negotiate a plan, the support of the lawyers is important. Often considerable pain is evident when the individuals realize that original goals must be modified. A natural tendency is to avoid or deny reality. The support and reality-oriented discussion with the lawyers may be necessary to ensure that the process reaches completion and that further litigation is avoided. In spite of all the efforts by the clinicians and lawyers, a small number of families may have to have their day in court, with decision making by court order.

Intervention Following Settlement of the Dispute

Ongoing contact with the family after the custody-access plan is determined is one of the more satisfying aspects of this work. One has the opportunity to see the storms pass and people relating to one another in a less tense, more cooperative, considerate manner. With the knowledge the clinician has of the family, new problems can often be resolved by brief interventions, avoiding resurgence of litigation.

If a shared or coparenting plan is not agreed to, then one parent will have the role of visiting parent. Out of hurt and loss of self-esteem, this parent may consider discontinuing contact with the children. Studies have reported extreme pain by visiting fathers (Grief 1979; Roman and Haddad 1978; Wallerstein and Kelly 1980). These feelings are exacerbated when the children appear reluctant or disinterested or even refuse visits, preferring to play with their friends, watch television, or even as one ten year old stated, "because I'm tired." Although at times there are realistic reasons requiring a change in the visiting time, the visiting or visited child also can feel pain in access visits. Guilt over the parent they leave, discomfort about the pain they sense in the absent parent, fear that either parent may ask questions about the other, or subtle pressure by the custodial parent may be acting to make visits uncomfortable. It takes much courage and perseverance to continue to pick up apparently reluctant or disinterested children and remain a loving parent. The clinician who maintains contact with the family in the early months of implementation of the custody and access plan may be very helpful in providing support, interpreting behavior, and offering guidance.

> *Harold, a concerned parent of three, faithfully picked up his children whenever it was allowed. Frequently his eldest daughter would misbehave or try to avoid visits in preference for other activities. Harold was deeply hurt and wondered if the visits were worth the effort. With the support of his therapist and interpretation of the possible meaning of the girl's behavior, he was able to maintain his constancy and not reject the girl.*

Invariably differences do occur that parents may not be able to resolve. Children have a tendency to present behavior that is perplexing and upsetting. Interpretation by the clinician may be helpful and diffuse conflict. Children may continue to be manipulative either in saying what they think the parents want to hear or, more commonly, by playing one against the other.

> *Mrs. Brown grounded her twelve-year-old daughter for poor behavior. The girl said she would not obey and was going to her father's. Unfortunately, although Mr. Brown knew what was happening, he allowed his daughter to come, completely undermining his former wife's discipline and leaving her realistically angry and the girl defiant.*

Deterioration in school performance is often seen but usually improves within two years (Wallerstein and Kelly 1980). The school and parents may find consultation useful. Discussion should center around how the children are faring and how to provide support without allowing the children to use the separation and their feelings about it to avoid responsibility.

Finances are a major stumbling block and may be the issue that destroys the best intentions and plans.

> *When Harold lost his job, his former wife was unsympathetic and unrelenting in her financial demands. She threatened, "No money, no kids." That she lived in a comfortable house and he in an empty apartment was no concern of hers. She was not prepared to take even part-time work, feeling it was her right to be supported as she had been in the past.*
>
> *Harold was able with guidance to remain involved with the children. Often he felt insecure and wondered if the children really cared and what impact he could possibly have on their lives. He began to revive old traditions and rituals. Religious celebrations were planned and made special events. Birthdays were honored. All of these were things not done in the mother's home. The difference in age between the*

children frequently created difficulty because the eldest did not enjoy the same activities as the youngest. Harold was supported in not always taking all three children on visits but in ensuring that he spent special time individually with each.

Because of his shame and depression, he had stopped seeing his former acquaintances and friends. Gradually he began to make contact, and his empty apartment no longer functioned as a place of safety where he could hide from the world. He began to bring friends in and resume a social life.

Currently the biggest problem remains finances. The support payments and legal debts take the majority of his earnings and make it almost impossible for him to create for himself a more comfortable life. Not surprisingly, at times he becomes discouraged and feels great resentment toward his former wife.

Most women are not as difficult as Harold's wife. Most go to work, often ill prepared with little education and unmarketable skills (Herzog and Sudia 1970; Colletta 1979; Desimone-Luis, O'Mahoney, and Hunt 1979; Brandwein, Brown, and Fox 1974; Jencks 1982). Sixty-nine percent of the Custody Project wives earned less than $10,000 as compared to 17 percent of the Custody Project's husbands. The single working father or mother feels overburdened and isolated. They worry about whether the children are being adequately supervised. Often they are so fatigued from the two jobs of work and home that they do not have time or energy to have fun with the children. Resentment may develop toward the absent parent, feeling he or she has all of the fun with few of the responsibilities.

Eventually many who divorce will become involved with a new partner or even remarry. The role the new partner should take regarding the children is almost always difficult to work out. Custodial parents may feel they must not burden the new partner with discipline. The absent parent may be resentful and jealous of the new partner's relationship with the children and the exspouse. He or she may be afraid of loss of love. It is important to counsel parents to let the new partner take on responsibilities regarding the children so that a true blending can occur, establishing a new functional family unit (Satir 1977).

The absent parent should be helped to see that his or her place is secure with the children and that there is no limit on the amount of love the child can have for others.

Other issues that may arise: the consequences of being a homosexual parent or one who is emotionally ill; alcoholism and violence in one or both parents; religious and moral differences; a parent having to move geographically; remarriage and new children. By being available, the clinician can provide information about the significance of these questions, helping the parents to institute the best possible plan under the circumstances. Sometimes feelings are aroused and old wounds reopened. It may be difficult to keep the important issues to the fore, and the clinician may have to be quite active to ease feelings to get problem solving again proceeding in a salutary direction.

Treatment

During assessment, it may emerge that some of the family members are emotionally disturbed and in need of treatment. In the project's sample, 60 percent of the parents had a diagnosable disorder. Therapy was recommended by the project clinicians for 8 percent of the mothers, 6 percent of the fathers, and 10 percent of the children. Family therapy was recommended for an additional 7 percent.

When individual therapy is needed, whether the assessing clinician undertakes to be the therapist is a question of timing and inclination. The essence of custody and access work lies in the clinician's maintaining and being seen as unprejudiced or neutral. When one steps into the role of therapist, this position is lost. The nature of the relationship between therapist and client must be explained since, if a later dispute over custody or access should arise, the clinician's previous role as a neutral mediation-assessment resource could not be regained. Further, the therapist's ability to maintain confidentiality under cross-examination in court could be in jeopardy.

When children have problems, referral to therapists with a family systems approach is advisable. Although children may have problems in their own right, the family exerts a major influence. Disturbance may be a manifestation of stress in the family system, such as incomplete resolution of loss or of the children's manipulating the parents and being out of control. Work may have to be done with both parents or with the whole family together. Many books and articles have been written about the problems of children of divorce and the process of therapy (Robson 1980; Tessman 1978; Despert 1962; Salk 1978; Hansen and Messinger 1982). Medical insurance will often cover the expenses of ongoing work with individuals or the family, which is a considerable aid to motivation, making help financially feasible.

One parent may not be as motivated to work for the good of the children. A clinician cannot cajole or force a reluctant parent to take responsibility. The reasonable parent may feel anger and resentment at seeing the children hurt. Therapy should focus on helping the motivated parent to avoid maligning the other and to allow the children to discover for themselves the characteristics of the other parent. The healthier parent should be encouraged to be supportive to the children, helping them to realize that it is not their fault that the parent does not visit or is unaccommodating. Nagging or lying to cover for the other parent does not help matters and may make it more difficult for the children to accept the reality of the situation. It may force the children to protect their idealized image of the erring parent.

There are groups available for the separated and divorced, some educational in focus, some social, and others therapeutic. The feeling of being isolated with few supports is well handled in groups where members have a chance to air feelings, receive advice, and learn that they are not alone.

Conclusion

Separation and divorce are processes that have a major impact on the constellation and function of the family. Most respond to the challenge of the crisis, finding strengths they did not know existed. For the rest, an approach that focuses on the child and the family, eliciting the most caring and considerate parts of all, should be sought. Ongoing conflict should be discouraged and everyone helped to complete the process of mourning the old life so that a new beginning can be made.

8
Clinical Issues in Custody Disputes

Ruth S. Parry
Elsa A. Broder
Elizabeth A.G. Schmitt
Elisabeth B. Saunders

By definition, separating and divorcing parents who are in conflict over the custody of their children constitute one subgroup of all separating and divorcing parents. Many couples, as they reach the decision to dissolve the marriage, develop a plan for their children to which both can commit. Implementation of the plan may occur in some families without the assistance of lawyers or clinicians. Others develop a plan and request assistance from lawyers to prepare a written separation agreement or minutes of settlement to be approved by a court. Another group, unable to devise a plan alone, is able to do so with the assistance of lawyers. Those couples who are more polarized in their positions about plans for the children comprise the group referred by counsel or the courts to mental health professionals. No data are available to describe the comparative size of these groups or their similarities or differences. Until needed research is completed, what knowledge we have is derived from subgroups of families known to some counseling resource. The authors' views were inevitably colored by the characteristics of the Custody Project's families.

In discussing clinical issues to be considered in working with families disputing custody of their children, this chapter will describe various kinds of custody arrangements as reported in the literature and, when possible, in relation to a known group of separating and divorcing families. Parent- and child-related factors found to be relevant to the mediation-assessment process with the Custody Project families will also be discussed.

Types of Custody Arrangements

Sole Custody

Weiss (1979b, p. 332) notes that no definition of custody exists in statute law and proposes the definition from *Words and Phrases* (1968):

Custody of a minor embraces the sum of parental rights with respect to the rearing of the minor and connotes a keeping or guarding of the child. It includes in its meaning every element of provision for the physical, moral, and mental well-being of the minor, including its immediate personal care and control.

Inherent in this definition is the win-or-lose concept; the parent having custody has every element in raising the child. This kind of custody arrangement is usually referred to as sole custody or exclusive custody and is the most frequently made court order.

Joint Custody

This term is generally accepted as referring to the legal guardianship and the care and control of children being the joint responsibility of both parents. Joint custody as a legal solution to disputed custody has been appealing to both the legal-judicial system and clinicians in that it can appear to lessen the win-or-lose aspect of a custody dispute. This legal arrangement may exist when the children are in the physical care and control of one parent, similar to a sole custody plan, but in law the right of the absent or noncustodial parent to participate in decision making about the child's future is protected.

Shared Parenting

When the physical and emotional care of the child is shared by both parents in a plan that is congruent with the child's needs and the realities of geographic location of both parents and their individual life circumstances, we term such a plan shared parenting.

Ideally a shared parenting plan would be required in a joint custody arrangement, although in practice this has not always been the case. It is our view that a shared parenting plan can be implemented by many families under a sole custody order providing adequate assistance is given to the family in gradually strengthening their negotiating ability. From the child's point of view, the degree of sharing by both parents in their lives is the important factor; the legal right to joint responsibility for the child's rearing is a parental concern. The mastery of shared parenting skills by separated parents can lay the foundation for a realistic joint custody plan. Thus, the Custody Project members support a joint custody plan by court order only in those situations in which shared parenting is an actuality.

Split Custody

This term has been variously defined as indicating placement of some children of the family with one parent and the other children with the other parent or as an arrangement in which on a preset time basis, the children reside alternately with one parent and then the other. The latter arrangement we view as inherent in a shared parenting plan; therefore, we use the term *split custody* when referring to the division of the children of the marriage between the separating or divorcing parents.

The split custody plan, like the joint custody plan that does not include actual shared parenting, must be considered with caution. When there are two or more dependent children, there is some risk that the awarding of custody of one child at least to each parent may in fact be based in each parent having "won" a child. Split custody plans are useful only in situations in which the relationship between the children is of low intensity or destructive and the attachment of each child to one parent is unusually strong.

Comparison of Arrangements

There has been extensive controversy as to which custody arrangement is best. Goldstein, Freud, and Solnit (1973) gave credence to the fact that factors other than physical care must be considered in deciding the placement of children. Drawing on psychoanalytic theory, they set as a basic premise "the need of every child for unbroken continuity of affection and stimulating relationships with an adult" (p. 6). They called into question "custody decisions which split the child's placement between two parents" (p. 6), suggesting that children should be placed with the psychological parent, whom they define as "one who, on a continuing, day-to-day basis through interaction, companionship, inter-play and mutuality fills the child's psychological needs for a parent, as well as the child's physical needs" (p. 98). This view implies that there is only one psychological parent to whom the child is attached, thereby supporting the traditional sole custody arrangement.

The literature on separation and divorce, the impact on parents and children, the effect of being raised in a single-parent home, which in most instances means a mother-led home, has increased rapidly over the past decade. The Custody Project members suggest, however, that it is a quantum leap to hold a preset preference for one or other custody arrangement based solely on generalizations from the few research studies available. Each individual family must be weighed on its own merits.

Consequences of Different Types of Custody Arrangements

The literature on the effects of different kinds of custody arrangements on parents and children is in its infancy, mainly because until the mid-1970s virtually all custody decisions awarded custody of minor children to the mother. Although mothers still usually obtain custody of their children, changes in the roles of men and women and changes in law pertaining to children and families have opened the way for other kinds of custody arrangements. In many U.S. states the exploration of the possibility of joint custody in divorce cases involving children is a mandatory requirement on the presiding judge; other states have passed laws in which the sex of the parent is not to be considered a decisive factor in determining custody (Benedek and Benedek 1972). The public debate as portrayed in the media, as well as in statements by professional associations, has focused on issues of joint custody and father custody in spite of the fact that only a small minority of separated families resolves the custody dispute through these arrangements. Much attention was generated in the mid-1970s when a prominent psychologist, Lee Salk, obtained custody of his children, arguing not that their mother was unfit but that he was equally capable of raising their children (Salk 1978).

Single-Parent Mothers and Their Children

The majority of children whose parents are separated live in the custody of their mothers for at least part of their growing-up years. Scientific interest in these children began in the 1940s and 1950s with studies on the effects of father absence on the development of perceptions of paternal behavior, sexual identification, and social competence in boys (Lamb 1976). In the 1950s and 1960s a great number of studies on father absence linked broken homes with all kinds of symptoms of maladjustment (Herzog and Sudia 1973). Depression, aggressive behavior, delinquency, academic difficulties, poor peer relationships, and marital difficulties in adulthood were found to occur more often in children from broken homes than in children growing up in intact families (Herzog and Sudia 1973). The late 1960s and 1970s witnessed a growing uneasiness with these studies, and questions regarding their methodology and the validity of their results were raised. More sophisticated methods of data collection and analysis led to criticisms of studies that included both children living with their widowed mothers and children of divorce into one group of children from broken homes and that failed to take into account differences in the mothers' socioeconomic class and parenting styles. By then broken homes had ceased to be exclusively the problem of the poor and were found in growing numbers in suburbs and affluent neighborhoods of big cities as well. The great number of children whose parents had separated and the heterogeneity of their socioeconomic background and family culture prior to their parents' divorce, the focus on the equality of women, particularly of middle-class women, made it increasingly more uncomfortable to use the findings of the father-absence studies and predict that all these mothers and children were doomed to social and psychiatric maladjustment.

New studies, larger in scale and often supported by large research grants, using methodologically sophisticated techniques of sample selection, data collection, and data analysis, were carried out. Reflecting the social climate of the 1970s, they were no longer called studies of father absence; rather their subject matter was referred to as the single-parent family in nonsexist language. However, the single-parent family research reported findings not too dissimilar to those of the father-absence studies: children being raised in single-parent families broken by separation rather than death of the father were again found to be more likely to show signs of social and emotional maladjustment (Brandwein, Brown, and Fox 1974).

By the late 1970s there was uneasiness with these studies as well. This time they were criticized for assuming that once socioeconomic class, race, and reason for the end of the parents' union (death or separation) were taken into account, all single-parent families were the same. In other words, such studies failed to look inside the family and investigate variables such as the mothers' emotional adjustment, parenting style, and support networks (Levitin 1979). Even this kind of criticism, however, could not dismiss the accumulating literature linking parental separation to difficulties in children's adjustment. The next fairly obvious question to arise was whether there are any factors that can mitigate the deleterious effects on children of family breakdown.

Current research is beginning to identify such factors. Single-parent mothers who are able to find emotional and financial stability, have sensitive, sound parenting practices, and are able to rely on relatives and/or friends for help with child-rearing and household management responsibilities raise children who at least on some measures of adjustment look no different from or even better than children from intact families (Herzog and Sudia 1973; Santrock and Warshak 1979).

The most obvious mitigating factor, however, is currently also the most controversial one. Children's pain about their parents' separation, if they remain in their mothers' custody, usually involves pain about losing daily contact with their fathers. Thus the question arises whether preserving the father–child relationship would lessen children's pain and inner turmoil following the parents' separation and prevent at least some of the deleterious effects of father absence.

The recent discovery of the postseparation father–child relationship and the controversy about its importance is not surprising if one considers that until the mid-1960s, the role of fathers in children's lives, even in intact families, had been overlooked by psychological theory and research, as well as by children's mental health services. Studies that have looked at the nature of father–child relationships following family breakdown found great variability in the frequency of contact between children and their noncustodial fathers, with some children continuing to see their fathers several times a week and others losing most or all contact with them either shortly after the separation or within the first two years following the breakup (Hetherington, Cox, and Cox 1976, 1978; Wallerstein and Kelly 1980).

The few studies reporting on children's wishes regarding custody arrangements and their relationships with their noncustodial parents indicate that many children long for ongoing contact with the other parent and suffer intensely if this relationship is severed or severely limited (Rosen 1979; Wallerstein and Kelly 1980).

Studies investigating relationships between single-parent mothers and their former husbands show great variability in their ability to maintain any kind of contact with each other and indicate sources of potential difficulty in preserving the father–child relationship for their children. Some separated parents maintain at least a polite and civilized relationship for their children's sake. They encourage their children to maintain a positive relationship with both parents. Some couples even continue to attend jointly parent–teacher meetings or to celebrate holidays together (Ahrons 1981).

Other separated parents' communications with each other are mainly conflictual, and no such continued cooperation is possible. Mothers who feel victimized by their former husbands, who do not receive support payments, or who see the father as exerting a negative influence on their children may try to limit or completely sever the children's relationship with the noncustodial father (Roman and Haddad 1978; Wallerstein and Kelly 1980). Fathers who feel that their wives make it difficult for them to see their children or who cannot tolerate the pain of seeing their children for only a few hours' visit, and then often under restricted conditions dictated by the custodial mother and/or a court order, may stop seeing their children. They report that such visits between themselves and their children are unsatisfactory and recreate or perpetuate the trauma of the separation for themselves and their children (Dominic and Schlesinger 1980; Hetherington, Cox, and Cox 1976). Further, some clinicians have been concerned that when contact between children and their fathers is colored by a hostile, mistrustful relationship existing between the two parents, it can undermine the custodial mother's authority and create instability and ongoing turmoil in the single-parent family unit and place the child in an intolerable loyalty conflict (Goldstein, Freud, and Solnit 1973).

Research on the development of children who live in their mother's custody has thus shown them to be a group of children at risk of maladjustment. Beyond this they have to be seen as a heterogeneous group in which some children are fortunate to have well-adjusted mothers and available fathers and others suffer the effects of their mothers' difficulties and/or their fathers' absence. Further, these children's initial negative reaction to their parents' separation may lead to behavioral and emotional problems in spite of adequate parenting (Hetherington, Cox, and Cox 1978). Thus, it can be the child's inability to adjust to the parents' separation that creates difficulties in his or her relationship to the custodial mother and in due course lead to a vicious circle of a disturbed child creating and then perpetuating a disturbed mother–child relationship (Hetherington, Cox, and Cox 1978).

Single-Parent Fathers and Their Children

Only a few studies have investigated single-parent fathers, a minority group, and their children's adjustment to this kind of custody arrangement (Chang and Deinard 1982). The findings presented here are only initial impressions and may have to be revised as more investigations of single-parent father-led families are carried out.

The data currently available indicate that fathers may be obtaining custody of their children under different circumstances than do mothers. Fathers appear to be more likely to obtain sole custody either after a prolonged custody dispute or when the mother relinquishes custodial claims (Gersick 1979; Luepnitz 1982; Watson 1981). Single-parent fathers may be slightly older and better educated and may have participated more actively during the course of the marriage in child-rearing tasks than have noncustodial separated fathers (Gersick 1979; Watson 1981). Interview studies usually find single-parent fathers reporting satisfaction with their custody arrangement and few problems with managing their household and child-rearing responsibilities (Bartz and Witcher 1978; Gasser and Taylor 1976; Smith and Smith 1981; Watson 1981).

Single-parent fathers may be more likely to utilize community resources and receive more support from their relatives and friends than do single-parent mothers (Hetherington 1983). This may be due to the fathers' greater financial means, which enables them to pay for help with child-rearing and household management tasks, as well as to people still perceiving single-parent fathers as particularly devoted parents deserving support, while single-parent mothers are expected to be able to cope with their children, households, and possible jobs as well by virtue of their womanhood (Hetherington 1983). Three comparative studies of children growing up in their mothers' and their fathers' custody found no differences in boys' self-esteem or in the behavior, psychosomatic problems, and school performance of children of both sexes (Lowenstein and Koopman 1978; Luepnitz 1982; Rosen 1979). Another study found that latency-age children show greater social competence, maturity, independence, and sociability when they were in the custody of the same-sex parent than in the custody of the parent of the opposite sex (Santrock and Warshak 1979). In other words, latency-age boys in their fathers' custody were found to show greater social competence than their peers growing up in their mothers' custody, while the reverse was true for the latency-age girls.

Joint Custody

Joint custody is the custody arrangement most favored by those who feel strongly that parental separation should not result in exclusion of one parent, usually the father, from the lives of the children (Grief 1979; Roman and Haddad 1978; Stack 1976).

Joint custody can take different forms, depending on whether the child remains living with one parent or alternates between the two parents' residences according to a prearranged schedule and depending on the degree of shared decision making between the parents. Interview studies with parents who maintain a joint custody arrangement indicate a high level of satisfaction (Abarbanel 1979; Grief 1979; Steinman 1981). At least one comparative study of mother custody, father custody, and joint custody has concluded that "joint custody at its best is superior to single-parent custody at its best" (Luepnitz 1982, p. 150). The advantages of a joint custody arrangement appear to be the preservation of the child's relationship with both parents, enabling both parents to continue to carry decision-making responsibility and thus to maintain an active involvement in guiding their children's development. The arrangement may avoid custody battles between parents who fear otherwise to lose their children and enable the two parents to rely on each other for relief and support with child-rearing tasks.

One rather important aspect, which not all proponents of joint custody address, can be the parents' mutual mistrust, hostility, and inability to communicate or agree on matters affecting their children's lives. One study found that relitigation of custody orders was lowest for parents who had a joint custody arrangement as compared with families in which a sole custody arrangement had been made (Ilfeld, Ilfeld, and Alexander 1982). The authors postulated that relitigation was likely to reflect continuing conflict between the parents, such conflict having been identified by other researchers as detrimental to the children. They concluded that joint custody may well be preferable to other arrangements. Forcing parents to carry joint decision-making responsibility in the face of such obstacles can mean perpetuating conflicts between them, perhaps exacerbating the conflicts that led to their separation in the first place. Another disadvantage is that this kind of custody arrangement can force both parents to remain in geographical proximity with each other and may make an emotional separation more difficult (Luepnitz 1981).

There are few data on children's reaction to a joint custody arrangement. It appears that children tend to appreciate maintaining contact with both their parents and that they tend to view this as an advantage that outweighs drawbacks such as frequent moves between homes and adjusting to two different sets of house rules (Abarbanel 1979; Leupnitz 1981; Steinman 1981). For some children, however, the complex schedules that they had to maintain in order to spend equal or close to equal time with each parent was confusing and burdensome, particularly if the two homes were at some distance from each other (Abarbanel 1979; Steinman 1981). While joint custody may be a workable arrangement for parents who respect each other and want to preserve their children's relationships with both parents, the details of this arrangement will need to vary according to the life circumstances of the parents and the age and needs of their children if it is to be a satisfactory solution to the breakup of the original family.

Guidelines for Intervention

Since 1976 the Custody Project members from their own experience, research, and the findings of others working with separating and divorcing families have evolved the following principles as a philosophic base for intervention:

1. Both separating parents should carry equal responsibility in ensuring that the least detrimental plan for the child's future is developed and implemented.
2. The child has the right to be heard with regard to his or her future custody or access plans, with the firm assurance that decision making lies in the hands of the adults and is not the child's responsibility.
3. The child has the right to the opportunity to maintain the most positive ongoing relationship possible with both parents following separation and divorce.
4. The process of mediation-assessment of a custody dispute must be child and family centered.

In working with families disputing child custody, the Custody Project members recognize that each family presents its own unique set of issues that must be considered in order to assist the parents in reaching an optimal plan for the custody of their children. Certain factors present sufficiently often that they can be identified to provide guidelines for the clinician, among them the following child-related factors:

1. Child's age, stage of development, and sex.
2. Quality of the child's attachment to each parent.
3. Child's preference or wish regarding custody planning.
4. Continuity of the child's care.
5. Attachment of the child to siblings.
6. Child's relationship to significant others.
7. Any special physical or emotional needs of the child.

The parent-related factors include the following:

1. Quality of the parent's attachment to the child.

2. Parenting style.
3. Parent's available time to spend with their child and their child-care plan.
4. Parent's emotional state and the impact of this on the child.
5. Parent's attitude to the other parent and ability to support the child's contact with the other parent.
6. Parent's new partner, if any, as a potential provider of care for the child.
7. Parent's support system.
8. Parent's religious persuasions.

Child-Related Factors

Child's Age, Sex, and Stage of Development. These three are the essential factors, against which all other child- and parent-related factors must be measured. Children's needs vary greatly at different ages and stages of development. Contrary to popular belief, younger children have more difficulty coping with the upheaval and stress of their parents' separation and divorce than do older children (Wallerstein and Kelly 1980). The maintenance of a stable, predictable home environment is particularly important for these younger children. Older children generally can tolerate more change.

The Custody Project study population included 215 children. Almost half were latency age, the remainder dividing almost equally between preschoolers and preadolescents and adolescent children. The data indicate no correlation between the age and sex of the child and the plan either mediated or recommended for the child's custody. More emphasis was placed on other factors, such as the nature of the psychological attachment between the parent and child (in 58 percent of cases), the child's expressed wishes (in 55 percent of cases), and the child's need for the continuity of care (in 49 percent of cases).

The child's stage of development became a more significant factor in custody planning when the child was viewed as manifesting developmental or behavioral problems. For example, if a three-year-old child expressed marked separation anxiety, the clinician on the basis of information and observation would discuss this with the parents. An inappropriate parental attitude to the child, impeding age-appropriate separation and individuation, would be considered an important deficit in the parenting capacity of that parent.

> *In the Gerrard family, each child developed a distinct response to the stress of the family's continued cohabiting but separate and apart. Janet, thirteen years old, responded by an exaggerated effort to separate and individuate in her early teens by aligning closely with a semide-*

linquent peer group. Stephen, ten years old and not developmentally ready to separate himself from his family, became overly anxious. Lisa, five years old, showed some regression and insecurity through increased attention seeking at home and at school, and Alice, eight years old, attempted mastery of the situation by becoming the family therapist.

Some children continue to function well with minimal symptoms in spite of the family turmoil. The parental separation did not appear to create or exacerbate emotional or behavioral problems in 67 percent of the children in the Custody Project population. The presence or absence of symptoms in children must be considered in the context of all factors in the situation.

Quality of the Child's Attachment to Parents. The Custody Project members cited this factor as being the one that influenced them most often in mediating or recommending a custody plan. As Goldstein, Freud, and Solnit (1973, p. 17) stated:

> For the child the physical realities of his conception and birth are not the direct cause of his emotional attachment. This attachment results from day-to-day attention to his needs for physical care, nourishment, comfort, affection and stimulation. Only a parent who provides for these needs will be able to build a psychological relationship to the child on the basis of the biological one and will become his "psychological parent" in whose care the child can feel valued and "wanted."

Thus the quality of the child's attachment to the parents is a reflection of the child's sense of his or her value in the parent's eyes. This attachment clearly is assessed by the clinician in various ways and not simply as a question related to the child's stated preference. It is possible that children have formed a strong bond to both their parents. It is also possible that they have bonded to neither parent but rather to a primary caretaker, such as a grandparent.

In the Gerrard family, the nature of the children's attachment to their parents varied. Janet vacillated in stating her preference. Her refusal to have contact with her father's girlfriend appeared to be based in loyalty to her mother and fear of loss of interest by her father in her. Stephen felt caught. It seemed that he appreciated that he received more comfort and understanding from his mother and yet had identified with his father's goals of academic and career achievement. Alice showed the clearest attachment to her mother. Lisa, the youngest, was unable to distinguish to which parent she was more attached, which in her case was likely realistic. Probably her strongest attachment was to her sibling group rather than to her parents, both of whom had exhibited such great personal difficulties during Lisa's life span that the opportunity had been absent.

Child's Preference or Wish Regarding a Plan. Of the Custody Project children, 67 percent expressed a clear wish for their own custody plan. The majority of the wishes expressed were viewed by the clinicians as representing the child's real wish rather than the parroted statement of Levy's "brainwashed" child (Levy 1978). It is important, though, for the clinician to assess the pressure on the child to state a wish. Forty-one percent of mothers and 39 percent of fathers did apply overt pressure of this nature.

Thirty percent of the children did not want to state a choice. The clinicians believed that 23 percent of those children did have a preference but that for these children, the loyalty conflict described by Goldstein, Freud, and Solnit (1973) was apparent. Thus, although many children did feel free enough to express a wish, these data support the view that it is imperative for children to know that the ultimate decision-making responsibility about their custody is not theirs but their parents' or the court's.

In expressing a wish, the children tended to respond as described by Wallerstein and Kelly (1980). The preschoolers responded with denial of the parental separation, the latency children responded with a rather rigid and moralistic judgment as to the good and the bad parent, and the adolescent children expressed a preference for the same-sex parent, although this was most evident in the adolescent girls.

Many children expressed as their first wish that their parents reunite. Thus their custody wish was actually second. The desire to have the parents reunite was strongest in the preschoolers and remained strong in the children as old as ten to twelve years. For most of the adolescent boys and girls, there was more acceptance of the parents' decision to separate. Some expressed the view that their parents needed to separate and that they felt relief following the separation.

Continuity of Child's Care. In 49 percent of cases, clinicians stated continuity of care as a major factor in the custody recommendations. The theoretical basis for this is strong and well documented in the vast literature on normal development and attachment theory (Spitz 1945; Bowlby 1973). In emphasizing continuity of care, the clinicians were placing primary importance on the child's need for stability and security. Young children have a very limited sense of space and time and have difficulty tolerating frequent changes in environment. Shared parenting plans must recognize this if stress for the young child is to be avoided.

Matthew, a three year old, was an only child. During his second year of life, his mother was repeatedly absent during brief extramarital affairs.

She then left permanently. Matthew's parents could not agree about his care. The court ordered that he spend half the week with his mother and half the week with his father. He showed various symptoms in response to this arrangement. At his mother's house, he was clingy and whining and had trouble sleeping. At his father's house, he was pseudo-mature, competing with his older cousins with whom his father lived. Both parents agreed that Matthew was suffering, but each was unwilling to diminish his or her time with Matthew.

For adolescents, continuity of care means something different. Often they have formed satisfactory attachments to both parents so the choice of custodial parent is not as important to them as maintaining their prior peer relationships and school stability.

There are some situations in which a change of custody may be indicated. These changes need not reflect the parent's ability to parent but rather reflect the child's changing needs. Many children, particularly girls, express a strong wish to live with the same sex-parent: others, after the custody plan has been established, express a strong wish to live with the other parent to make more realistic their own internalized image of that parent. In other instances, the children may wish to be reunited with their sibling group or become part of a new family. The other parent may have remarried and even have a child by the new union, leading to the child in custody of a single parent wishing to become part of the new family unit despite a strong attachment to the current custodial parent. Some families are flexible enough to allow changes in custody to occur smoothly.

Martha, a nine year old, was very strong-minded. Three years earlier when her parents had separated, she had remained in the custody of her mother. Subsequently her father married a woman with children of her own. Martha increasingly wanted more and more time with her father and his new family. This created behavioral difficulties between herself and her mother. In response to his daughter's strong statement that she wanted to live with him, the father reopened the issue of custody with his former wife.

Despite the clinicians' perception of Martha as a strong-willed and possibly omnipotent child, the clinician also recognized her desire to be part of a family. Martha described vividly the warm, loving atmosphere she perceived at her father's house with lots of group participation and family chats. This was in constrast to her somewhat lonely and isolated life with her mother. Custody to father was recommended; however, the prediction was also made that when Martha reached early adolescence, she might wish to return to live with her mother. In the meantime, frequent access was wanted by Martha and her mother and supported by her father.

Attachment to Siblings. Clinicians cited attachment to siblings as being a major factor in 23 percent of their recommendations. Siblings can form a mutual support group, which helps them cope with the turmoil of their parents' separation. In 30 percent of the Custody Project families, the children stated that they wanted to remain with their siblings; for 10 percent, like the Gerrard children, remaining together had more importance for them than the choice of custodial parent. The intensity of attachment in the sibling groups of this subgroup of children was extremely high.

> *The Millers had three boys, a nine year old, a seven year old, and a five year old. Their marriage had been stormy for about five years prior to the separation. At the time of the assessment, both parents continued to cohabit, separate and apart, because neither wished to give up custodial rights, and both felt the other parent would have a damaging influence on the children. The boys had a different perspective. They had concerns for each other as well as for their parents. The eldest, James, was closely aligned with his father and wanted to live with him. Phillip, the seven year old, felt the most torn. He shared his mother's zest for life and yet was closely attached to his older brother, to the point of idealizing him. James had been an effective surrogate father to him as long as he could remember. Peter, the youngest, although he related well to his brothers, showed a strong need to reside with his mother. Both parents were considered capable of providing adequate parenting. This dilemma was resolved by recommending split custody, with the older boys living with their father and the youngest with his mother. All three boys continued to attend the same school, and after school they were cared for by the same babysitter in order to support their strong sibling ties.*

Child's Relationship to Significant Others. In several of the Custody Project families, other people besides the parents were very significant to the children. These included the extended family members, neighbors, and school friends. As well, teachers, recreational groups, and others providing daily care, such as nannies, day care center staff, and regular babysitters, were important. When both parents were employed, such people held an even greater significance for the child. In roughly 5 percent of the families, custody recommendations included extended family, such as grandparents, as primary caretakers. In a few cases, full guardianship was given to these extended family members on the basis that these people had a more significant relationship to the child than did the parents.

Special Physical or Emotional Needs. A small number of the Custody Project children had special needs. Some children, like Stephen Gerrard, had learning disabilities and consequently needed special education programs. Thirty-nine percent of the boys and 24 percent of the girls were viewed as suffering from emotional disturbance. The willingness and the ability of the parent to obtain the necessary help for the child influenced the recommendations for a custody plan.

> *Although Stephen Gerrard's learning difficulties had been extensively investigated and a remedial program established, Mr. Gerrard's need for his children's academic success was so intense that he denied Stephen's difficulties and insisted on a level of academic performance that Stephen could not meet. In contrast, Mrs. Gerrard worked closely with the school personnel to support Stephen's remedial program.*

Parent-Related Factors

Quality of the Parent's Attachment to the Child. This factor, in combination with the quality of the child's attachment to the parent, is the primary factor cited by the Custody Project clinicians in their recommendations regarding custody. There are many different ways that parents can express an attachment to their children, from open displays of affection to recognition of the child's individual personality with its pleasing and displeasing characteristics and a sincere concern for the child's needs. For most parents, the child represents to some degree an extension of themselves. Most parents want custody in an appropriate way; that is, they want to be actively involved in nurturing and guiding the child.

A few parents perceived the child as primarily an extension of themselves. They were unable to distinguish the child's needs as being separate from their own and therefore could not allow the child to separate and individuate appropriately. Clinically these families were difficult because sometimes the child was so enmeshed with one parent that he or she could not tolerate either interviews alone or interviews with the other parent. The clinical dilemma was whether to separate forcibly the child from the pathogenic parent. Usually, unless a delusional system was involved in the parent, project members did not provoke a separation but rather attempted treatment.

Some parents viewed custody as a means of expressing anger toward the other parent. In these cases, the children were used as angry inquisitors to chide or report about the other parent. The latency-age children were particularly vulnerable to parental pressure to take sides. For other parents, the issue of financial responsibility weighed heavily. Some perceived having custody as being less financially burdensome than support payments would be. Not uncommonly, parents perceived custody of the children as a contest in which the winner would obtain both the children and the matrimonial home. This perception of the situation did not negate the fact that these same parents may have genuinely cared for their children. Yet the win–lose flavor of the custody contest skewed the parents' ability to see the children's needs clearly.

> *Mildred and Paul Wheeler had been married for thirteen years. Both had worked initially. When the first child arrived ten years later, Mrs. Wheeler became a professional mother. She said she knitted and baked and joined a church group and the home and school group. Four children later, she began to resume her nursing career part time. Mr. Wheeler was opposed to her working, complaining that she had lost interest in the children and the home. He had not had a university education but instead had a trade. By hard work and taking extra courses, for which Mildred often typed his papers, he had gained enough credits to become a teacher. He had been able to buy a modest house in a small town, comfortable enough for four children.*
>
> *When Mildred decided that she wanted to break free of the marriage because she found Paul markedly overcontrolling, Paul was devastated. He had worked hard to support his family and had just one year to go to pay off the mortgage. At the point of separation, Mrs. Wheeler had wanted him to leave the home. He refused, so she left and sued for custody and possession of the home until the children were raised. Mr. Wheeler was convinced that if he gave up custody of the children, he would have lost everything. He cared dearly for the children and had in fact adequately managed as a single parent during the six months since Mrs. Wheeler had left the home. He threatened that if he lost custody, he would not be able to afford to pay support and to maintain a suitable dwelling for himself in which he could have his children even for overnight access.*

Parenting Style. This factor is difficult to define. Each clinician appeared to have a strong sense of what styles of parenting best suited a particular child's temperament. When the clinicians were asked to state why they felt one parent was less able than the other as a custodial parent, parenting style was an important reason given for 15 percent of the mothers and 21 percent of the fathers.

Clearly this factor is vulnerable to the greatest degree of subjective bias on the part of the clinician. Descriptions of parenting style of the Custody Project parents varied widely: consistent–inconsistent, permissive–overcontrolling, rigid–flexible, intrusive–distant. The concept of the complimentarity of the parent's and child's personality styles related to this factor, as did the parent's awareness of the child's perceptions and needs. Flexibility of parenting styles in response to the child's changing needs was deemed important.

Mr. and Mrs. Braun separated when their only child, Tommy, was fourteen months old. By agreement Tommy remained in his father's care. A liberal access plan was agreed to but unreliably utilized by Mrs. Braun until Tommy was four years old. At that time, Mr. Braun formed a common-law union. Mrs. Braun was surprised, having expected that at some point she and Mr. Braun would reunite. She applied to the court for increased access on a three times a week basis. Mr. Braun responded with an application for decreased access with preset arrangements in part to avoid contact between Mrs. Braun and his new partner. Mrs. Braun's previous lack of reliability in visiting Tommy was an important factor. Of greater concern was her infantilizing of Tommy. Mrs. Braun's need to deny Tommy's age-appropriate mastery of skills in dressing and feeding himself and her fostering of regressive infantile behavior were viewed as factors leading to a period of structured access supervised by the clinician.

Parent's Available Time to Spend with Their Child and Their Proposed Child-Care Plan. For almost all of the Custody Project families, separation or divorce resulted in financial pressure. This meant that both parents often had to be employed. In turn, this meant that the parents had to develop some plan for the care of the child in their working hours, some time for them to be with the child, and some time for themselves. Clinicians noted not only the amount of time the parent had available to be with the child but also how the time was used. For only 3 percent of mothers and 12 percent of fathers was there concern that the parents had not planned adequate time for their children. In these instances, the problem appeared to be the parents' questionable motivation in wanting custody rather than a lack of free time.

The child-care plans arranged varied widely, often including imaginative and creative options for the children. Those plans that allowed for maximum contact between the absent parent and the child were encouraged. The following example describes one situation in which a previously successful shared parenting plan had to be altered.

Jody, age three, was an only child, born six years after her parents' marriage. They separated when she was eleven months old, both parents in agreement with the shared parenting arrangement. This worked well until her mother established residence in a small town 300 miles away from the father. The parents maintained the shared parenting arrangement with considerable difficulty. Then each applied for sole custody. Pending referral for clinical assessment, the court ordered a continuation of the shared parenting arrangement on an interim basis. This required that Jody be transported twice weekly between the parents, the mileage totaling over 1,200 miles a week for the parents and 12 hours a week of travel time for Jody. Both parents reported behavioral signs of stress in Jody with this arrangement. They recognized that although the weekly shared parenting plan had been feasible while they lived in the same city, it clearly became destructive to their child's development following the mother's change in residence.

Parent's Emotional State. The Custody Project data on the parents' psychiatric histories and current emotional state indicate that in 72 percent of the families, at least one parent was seen as psychiatrically disturbed. For over half of the mothers and fathers, previous psychiatric contacts had been with regard to problems during the marriage or reaction to the marital breakdown. The Custody Project members found that the pressure of psychiatric disorder did not necessarily result in a poor parent–child relationship or inadequate parenting. The parent's emotional disturbance became relevant when it was involving of the child, interfering with the child's development, blocked the parent's ability to perceive the child as a separate person, or was basic to the parent's intractably negative view of the other parent.

Mrs. Gerrard had sought psychiatric help for depression and listlessness. Following the notification from her husband of his petition for divorce, she made a serious suicidal attempt. Both of her symptoms were related to the marital tension and only indirectly involving of the children. Thus, Mrs. Gerrard's ability to care for the children actually improved after treatment and with her release from the strain of the marriage.

Parent's Attitude to the Other Parent. When parents were able to agree on a plan for custody and access arrangements for their children, their attitude toward one another's parenting ability was mainly positive, although some differences of opinion on child-rearing methods might remain. In families in which a mediated plan could not be achieved, the parents remained preoccupied with the events or conflicts that they perceived as leading to the marital breakdown.

The children were all too aware of these entrenched negative attitudes. They witnessed their parents' harassment of each other, at times to the degree that one charged the other with allegations of child abuse or assault. It seemed that when one parent was either ambivalent about the separation or had a strong wish to reconcile, then the accusations became more severe, and the children were placed more overtly in the position of being asked to choose sides. Not only does such bitterness in itself cause stress for the child and undermine the child's need to respect both parents, but also the child is pressured to examine his or her own identification with the other parent and to reject those aspects of self that reflect internalization of that parent's values. Denigration by one parent of the other is one of the most harmful outcomes of separation and divorce for children. This parental behavior can lead to depression in the child, with all of its behavioral equivalents.

A major goal in counseling parents is to persuade them to cease their quarrel, particularly if it involves the children. To their credit, 27 percent of the Custody Project parents encouraged their children to express their own wishes about custody planning and did not ask them to take sides. In intractable disputes, the children became messengers of anger between their parents. The children then were vulnerable to feeling much guilt and to being convinced that they were responsible for their parents' distress. When these disputes could not be mediated, Custody Project members tended to recommend custody to the parent who was the more accepting of the child's relationship with the other parent.

Parent's New Partner. At the time of contact with the families, one-third of the fathers and mothers had become involved in another union. The new partners affected the custody dispute in the perceptions of all family members. Often the parents perceived only the negative side of the other parent's new union. Brown (1976, p. 423) pointed out that "early re-marriage is one of the biggest threats to successful divorce." The parent entering a new marital relationship may have done so as a means of coping with loneliness and low self-esteem following the family breakdown. The psychological investment in the new partner in such situations often appeared to be extraordinarily intense. As Kaslow (1981) notes, a new union may reactivate old conflicts between the parents that had been progressing toward resolution until the new partner's arrival.

Children often have a different perception of a new partner. They may perceive the partner as an obstacle to their wish for parental reunion; all the jealousies and disappointments that stepparents present in fairy tales may become acted out. On the other hand, children may be relieved to see the parent happy again, particularly when the new relationship is stable and if the new partner is responsive to the children's needs.

Some children actively seek an intact family, wanting to be in that environment again. They may have perceived themselves as getting in the way of their parents' finding someone new. When they see their parents getting support from other adults rather than primarily from themselves, they can again become children.

Parent's Support System. The presence of a solid support system for a parent is particularly important as each experiences the strain of separation. Friends who will babysit or simply be supportive and relatives who will be understanding and accepting can assist the individual to mobilize his or her energies to parent constructively. The children also will be aware of the constructive or destructive impact of the people who are significant to the parents.

Parent's Religious Themes. Although the Custody Project did not collect data on this factor, in a number of the families, disagreement about the religious unbringing of the children was presented as an emotionally charged issue. Some families held particularly intense religious beliefs. In these families, the stated reason for the marriage was usually that both partners believed that the other held the same intense religious beliefs. A primary factor in the marital breakdown was that one broke the faith, and much bitterness and venom ensued. In these situations, moralistic rationales were offered to support custody claims. The children were also pressed with moralistic arguments, forcing an alignment with one or other parent because compromise was not possible. At times, where the religious affiliation was to a particularly close knit and rigid group, the whole religious community also ostracized one parent. The children then felt forced to deny any positive feelings felt toward that parent. Although representing a small number of families, these situations were particularly unresponsive to mediation efforts.

Special Situations

Severe Mental Illness. Few of the parents suffered from a major mental illness, such as a psychosis. When the child had become incorporated into a parent's delusional system, custody was definitely contraindicated. In such a case, the child may have been strongly attached to the disturbed parent, yet the degree of pathology indicated that severing this bond was the only means by which the child could have the opportunity to live in a normal environment. In other families, though the parent may have experienced a severe illness, he or she may also have sought appropriate treatment and been able to make wise plans for the children.

> *Anne and Bobby, ages ten and seven, had been in their mother's interim custody since their father left the home. The marital separation was mutually agreed to by the parents; however, the father applied for custody on the basis that his wife had had three psychotic episodes requiring hospitalization during the fifteen years of marriage. The mother had been on medication throughout those years and had stabilized well in between episodes that had occurred prior to the marriage and after each child's birth. The mother had been clear in her explanation of her illness and had had firm support from her relatives when she needed assistance in caring for the children in the home. She demonstrated good judgment in the past in seeking assistance when she felt that her functioning was deteriorating.*

Mr. and Mrs. Martin were contesting custody of their eight-year-old daughter, Mary. Initially Mr. Martin had agreed that his wife have custody and requested frequent access for himself. Two years after the separation, he learned from Mary that his wife was increasingly reluctant to allow Mary to go out of the home other than to school. Background information indicated that Mrs. Martin had been raised in extremely sheltered circumstances. Her acquaintanceship with Mr. Martin was brief prior to the conception of Mary, and this led to their marriage. Mrs. Martin's long-standing suspiciousness had developed into a paranoidal system in which she perceived Mary as being at risk of sexual molestation whenever the girl was away from home. Mary was beginning to incorporate her mother's fearfulness.

Intrafamilial Violence. In 62 percent of the families, allegations of intrafamilial violence were made. When the violence occurred between the spouses only and did not involve the children, the clinical impression was that the allegations were highly exaggerated. In one family, the wife had charged both her husband and her father with a total of seventeen charges of assault. All the charges were subsequently dismissed. Her father became her major emotional and financial support. Usually the allegations were that the husband had beaten the wife. In a few families, the wife had beaten the husband, and in others, both partners had been physically abusive of the other. In three cases, there were allegations of violence against the child only. Investigation did not substantiate these allegations; rather, one parent was attempting to undermine the credibility of the other parent.

In 16 percent of the Custody Project families, allegations of violence by the fathers against both the mothers and the children were made. These allegations were found to be the most accurate. Only one of these fathers received custody of the children. In that situation, the father's violence was on one occasion only, his parenting skills were generally good, and he had sought counseling for himself and assistance for the children and himself as they adjusted to being a single-parent family.

Sexuality Issues. A sensitive area for people experiencing marital breakdown is concern around their own personal self-esteem and their sexual competence. The fact of the separation or the divorce may mean to them a failure in mate selection. In some situations, the grounds for the divorce were either adultery or homosexuality. In the project families, many couples referred to either their own or their partner's extramarital affairs as one of the problems leading to their separation. In some families, the legal affidavits included details about the sexual behavior of the other partner. These issues frequently were stated in a highly moralistic and emotional manner. The clinicians considered the important point to be the parent's ability to keep his or her sexual life separate from child rearing. Often the children had met the parent's partner, and sometimes they quite liked that person. Rarely had the parents allowed their children to witness sexual acts.

In a few families, allegations were made of incest between father and daughter. These allegations were treated carefully. In some cases, the clinician found no supporting evidence. In other cases, there was reason to believe that incest might have occurred. The child welfare authorities were then notified to investigate.

Nontraditional sexual behavior on the part of a parent did not in itself contraindicate custody; other factors were considered. Homosexuality in Canadian law is one ground for divorce, and it may be used as a reason to withhold custody from the other parent. Money, Hampson, and Hampson (1957) and Stoller (1968) have shown that core gender identity is established by age three. The way in which a child develops sexual object choice later is less clearly understood; however, many homosexual adults have come from two-parent families in which neither parent was homosexual. Thus the presence of a heterosexual parent did not prevent the child from making their alternate choice. Much more important to the child's needs is the nature of the child–parent bond and the parents' ability to separate their sexual life from their life with the child.

Summary

From the review of the current literature and the findings from the research data, the gaps in the available knowledge of decision making in custody disputes become apparent. Most studies have considered only one or two aspects of the separation and divorce process. No cross-sectional view of divorcing families has been available. All revere the theme of the best interests of the child, yet each research study and clinical resource comes to somewhat different conclusions as to what are the major factors in reaching custody decisions. In the Custody Project's study, the quality of the child's attachment to the parent, the child's wishes, and the need for continuity of care were cited by clinicians most frequently as being the primary factors that influenced their custody recommendations. Surprising, even to the project members, was the finding that contrary to the current trend for custody to be awarded to mothers, the data indicate that in this population, mothers and fathers equally often were recommended to be the custodial parent, independent of either the age or the sex of the child. The project clinicians considered many factors in their decisions. They placed more emphasis on the child-related factors than on the parent-related factors. The parents were encouraged to place their needs second to their children's needs, recognizing the relative helplessness and dependency of the children.

Further research is clearly necessary. The validity of the guidelines require testing. A prospective study could help define much more accurately how decision making is influenced.

9
Clinical Issues in Access Disputes

George Awad
Elizabeth A.G. Schmitt

In the history of the Custody Project, the resolution of access disputes has been the most difficult. Too often, once the decision regarding custody has been made, the courts and the custodial parent feel the conflict has been solved. Yet it is the ability to negotiate as reasonable access as possible that will dictate both the child's and the parents' ultimate adjustment to the marital breakdown. The separated parents need to continue a cooperative relationship for the sake of the child, with no win-or-lose criteria. This cooperation is frequently difficult to achieve.

In this study, 17 percent of the families were referred for assessment of access disputes only. In all of the custody assessments, arrangements for access also needed to be addressed. Specific access recommendations were made in 71 percent of the total study sample. The project members held the basic belief that a child requires a relationship with two parents for optimal emotional and social growth. The issue then became how to negotiate the best possible arrangement for the child given the personalities of the family members, their areas of conflict, and the practical occupational, geographical, and financial limitations with which the families had to deal. Whereas members of the project recommended a change in existing custody arrangements for only 28 percent of families, they recommended that existing access arrangements change in some way for 68 percent of families.

Definitions

For the purpose of this chapter, *access* will be defined as the legal arrangement by which the noncustodial or absent parent visits with the child or children of the marriage following separation or divorce. Usually access involves the biological or adopted children of the marriage; however, stepchildren may be included. As well, the term *access* usually refers to the parent's access or visitation rights, yet the rights of grandparents, aunts, and uncles were often considered an important factor, particularly when significant emotional bonds with the child existed. In a few cases, the grandparents had actually been the primary caretakers of the children, either because both parents worked or because of a parent's emotional instability or immaturity. In one case, the maternal aunt and uncle had played a significant role in rearing the child. This couple applied for custody following the death of the child's natural mother. Although the father retained custody, ongoing contact with the aunt and uncle was an important factor in meeting the child's needs. In a few cases where the parents were intransigent in their own conflict, denial of access by the noncustodial parent seemed unavoidable, yet ongoing access between separated siblings was still considered.

The legal-judicial system uses a variety of terms to define various access plans. A liberal access arrangement implies that the parents will decide together in a mutually cooperative fashion what the access arrangements are to be. These may include evening visits for dinner, regular weekend visits, summer holiday times, and cooperative sharing of time should one parent be out of town or during a parent's vacation or illness. When liberal access is supported by both parents, they consider the needs of the child—that is, the child's need to retain an ongoing, flexible relationship with both parents while maintaining normal activities with peers—as paramount. Participation of both parents in making medical decisions, attending teacher's interviews, and participating in other activities is possible and encouraged. Philosophically Custody Project members believe that whenever possible, this position is to be preferred. This approach resembles that defined as shared parenting in that the parents are mutually supportive in parenting. They participate actively in the education, health care, and religious training of the child and the child's normal activities. However, the role of custodial parent is clearly assigned in the minds of all. The recommendation for liberal access was made in 41 percent of the project cases. A liberal access plan requires sufficient flexibility in the separated family system to accommodate to the changing needs of the child and the parents.

For many conflicted couples, the choice of liberal access is too difficult to negotiate. Instead they require a more rigidly outlined arrangement, whereby each parent's role is spelled out in detail. This option is termed structured access. There are specific rules regarding visiting, including specific times for pickup and return home of the child. Clear specifications for summer vacations, school holidays, and other special events such as Christmas and birthdays are made. Specific plans requiring coordination of the parents for babysitting, educational tutoring, telephone calls, and medical visits may be included. The child's needs are paramount in drawing up such a plan. However, the tenuous quality of the parents' ability to negotiate implies that there may be a risk of breakdown of the access arrangements when changes must be made, whether due to the changing needs of the children or the parents. Ongoing mediation may be recommended for these families to enable them to adapt to or even prepare for the inevitable changes requiring alteration of access arrangements. In 27 percent of the project families, a structured access plan was developed.

More restrictive arrangements are termed supervised access and limited access. In supervised access, a third party, such as an extended family member or child care worker, is involved during the visit to ensure the child's emotional and physical safety. The duration of a supervised access plan must be short term, with a goal of assessing the viability of an ongoing structured access arrangement. The pragmatic difficulties in ensuring third-party supervision of access are great. The plan acknowledges either the possibility of inadequate child care by the visiting parent or such severe ongoing conflict between the parents that their contact at the point of pickup or return may be damaging to the child. Limited access is a plan in which the visits occur only two or three times a year. In one family the parents were separated by the Atlantic Ocean. The child visited her paternal grandparents regularly because they lived near the custodial mother's home. The child visited her father twice yearly. In another family, custody was granted to the paternal grandparents, who carefully controlled the access of the child, then age five, to both natural parents. In this situation, access to the natural mother was limited to two occasions a year. Somewhat more frequent access was available for the natural father.

Access between a child and a noncustodial parent is supported whenever possible. The objective is to find the access arrangement that will be the least disruptive to the child's sense of continuity in life and that will promote as strong a relationship as possible with both parents. To achieve this when liberal access is not possible, the more unusual plans of supervised access and limited access have been utilized. Yet there are situations when access must be denied. Because very special circumstances are involved in making such a recommendation, denial of access will be addressed separately.

Literature Review

Very little has been written specifically on the topic of access. Perhaps the reason is that access arrangements are more difficult to establish and are more susceptible to breakdown than are custody arrangements. The literature on access can be divided into two types: theoretical discussion based on clinical impressions (Group for the Advancement of Psychiatry 1980; Goldstein, Freud, and Solnit 1973; Roman and Haddad 1978) and, more recently, studies of access following marital separation (Ahrons 1980, 1981; Dominic and Schlesinger 1980; Hetherington 1979).

The work of Goldstein, Freud, and Solnit (1973) is the best known and the most controversial. They state that if the child's best interest is to be served, placement of the child, even following divorce, must not be conditional. In addition, they feel that children have difficulty in relating positively to, or benefiting from, or maintaining contact with two psychological parents who are not in positive contact with each other. Although these loyalty conflicts are viewed as common and normal under conditions of parental estrangement, they may have devastating consequences in destroying the child's positive relationship to each parent. These authors believe that a noncustodial parent has little chance to serve as a true object for love, trust, and identification because this role is based on the parent's being available on an uninterrupted day-to-day basis. Consequently, they recommend that the noncustodial parent should have no legally enforceable right to visit the child and that the custodial parent should have the right to decide whether it is desirable for the child to have visits with the absent parent.

These concepts gave rise to interprofessional polemic. There are those who state (Grief 1979) that not only is access a parental right and desirable for both parents and children but that divorce should not make any change in the parental relationships with children. To ensure this, some authors have advocated the concept of joint custody whereby the parents would continue in law to share equally the responsibility for the child's upbringing. The child may be in the care and control of one parent or alternating between the parents' homes. The time spent by each parent with the child may vary greatly or be so liberal as to amount to shared parenting.

While many theoretical papers and books have been written about joint custody, perhaps the most representative is Roman and Haddad's book, *The Disposable Parent* (1978). The authors present a lengthy review of the literature to stress their thesis that both parents are essential to the child's upbringing. They strongly dispute the claim of Goldstein, Freud, and Solnit that the noncustodial parent would not have a chance to serve as a true object for the child and recommend joint custody as the preferred plan for most separating families.

A third group of authors has taken a middle ground (Awad and Parry 1980; Benedek and Benedek 1977). These authors do not accept Goldstein, Freud, and Solnit's assumption that the child needs a continuous and unconflicted relationship with only one parent. Instead they feel that the child benefits from maintaining a relationship with both parents. Thus, access is viewed as a child's right that should be maintained and encouraged. These authors do not subscribe to the universality of joint custody, however, particularly when it involves frequent residence change for the child in order to maintain a program of equal time with each parent. They enunciate a principle of as liberal access as possible, with changes in residence determined by the child's age and stage of development. They believe that so many factors enter into the determination of access that there is no ideal access plan. Instead, each access plan should take all factors into account on a case-by-case basis.

In the past few years, a few studies have included an investigation of access and its effect on children (Hetherington, Cox, and Cox 1976; Wallerstein and Kelly 1980). The one common finding of these studies is that the noncustodial parent can continue to be a significant object for the children. In addition, children who have been allowed to maintain contact and a relationship with both parents have fared better developmentally than have children who have been denied such a contact. Wallerstein and Kelly (1980) found that access for a significant number of children continued to have potential for increasing the closeness and affection between the child and the noncustodial parent. They felt that such a relationship could transcend the anger and the instability of the separated family structure and that brief clinical intervention was a factor in the continuity of positive relationships between the child and both parents.

Clinical Issues in Considering Access

Because access involves ongoing interaction between the separated or divorced parents, it can be both the source of and vehicle for continuing conflict between them. Custody is more concrete and involves one decision that is most often associated with physical residence. Many parents do not contest custody, and of those who do, clinical intervention and/or a court order usually resolves the issue. The same cannot be said about access. In addition, continuing conflict between the parents may be displaced onto the access dispute.

When clinicians assess an access dispute, they usually have a frame of reference and some guidelines regarding access. This may vary from a flexible shared parenting arrangement to absolute sole custody. Both positions have merit, but Custody Project clinicians believe that neither should be a presumption. Instead, the basic principle held by the Custody Project members is that access is a child's right, not a parent's right. Making the child's right paramount is a reflection of the fact that the child is dependent and is in need of the best possible environment to ensure his or her growth and development. Conversely, parents are assumed to be adults who can fend better for themselves. They are responsible for the marriage and the separation and should not place the children in the position of having to choose between them following the marital breakdown. The amount and kind of access are determined by the degree of benefit accruing to the child rather than to the parents. It should not be assumed that access is an inalienable right of the parents. In the vast majority of situations, access is routinely expected and is constructively carried out for both children and parents. In certain situations, however, the parents should be required to earn access.

Advantages of Access

From their clinical experience and research findings, the Custody Project members concur with the findings of others that access to the noncustodial parent is beneficial to the child. This finding has at times been misinterpreted to mean that unlimited access is preferable or that joint custody is the preferred plan in all situations. Undisputed and flexible access is the result of many factors in the parents and the children, and it is an indication of healthy parental functioning. This finding, however, should not be interpreted to mean that children who do not have access to the absent parent would do better if access were imposed. Imposed access is likely to increase the tension between conflicted parents, with a resulting negative impact on the child.

Access is beneficial and desirable and may be expected in most families. One important reason for ongoing access is that it maximizes the child's chances for optimal development due to the continuing influences of both parents. Maintaining access is the only way to provide a child with the opportunity for a relationship with both parents. We recognize that the earlier focus on the exclusive role of the mother in child development and psychopathology is not correct. Although the influence of the mother on the child is central, the role of the father is not peripheral. The father plays a major role in the development of both boys and girls at all developmental stages. This has been the subject of several recent psychoanalytic studies and observations (Burlingham 1973). Further, the interrelationships between children in a family are important in each child's development, an aspect of separation and divorce that has received little attention.

The statement that fathers play an important role in the child's development does not suggest that access will maintain the relationship with both parents as though separation has not occurred. Although some visiting parents maintain a superficial and indulgent relationship with their children, many parents work hard after separation to maintain a realistic relationship. Even if visiting is not the optimal situation for maintaining such a relationship, the alternative would be single-parent families with one unavailable parent. A number of studies and observations, however, show that single-parent mothers—and the great majority of single-parent families are headed by women—are often beset by problems such as financial stress and task overload that have a negative influence on parenting ability and can lead to conflicted mother–child relationships and adjustment difficulties in the children (Herzog and Sudia 1970; Levitin 1979).

Access is beneficial to children because it prevents the occurrence of potentially pathological situations in two ways. First, the presence of the second parent will allow the child to interact with an important object in reality rather than in fantasy. Although the interaction with a weekend parent might not be as ideal as interacting on a day-to-day basis, it is better than no interaction. If the noncustodial parent is not available, the child will fantasize about him or her. The image of the parent will not be realistic since it is based on old memories of the child or the projection, often negative, of the custodial parent and affected by the current developmental needs of the child. In addition, the child may have egocentric and self-blaming explanations for the absence of the parent. A visiting parent would help the child integrate his or her self and object representations on a more realistic basis. Second, visiting prevents the child from experiencing the parental separation as a complete object loss. Research findings from studies comparing father loss by death, desertion, or prolonged absence indicate that the effect on the child of the loss has some similarities in all three situations. Several authors (Tuckman, and Regan 1966; Santrock 1975; and Hetherington 1972) concur in their findings that children from divorced families have more problems with aggressive and antisocial behavior, whereas children experiencing father loss through death are more likely to manifest anxiety, moodiness, and neurotic symptoms. That loss of a father may constitute a major developmental interference is not in doubt.

There are also practical reasons why children with access do better than children without. Separating parents are under stress and may not be able to provide adequately for the child. Thus, the sharing of the responsibility between parents provides more for the child's needs. Visiting provides relief time and financial savings in babysitting expenses for the custodial parent. In addition, the more involved the noncustodial parent is with the child, the more likely he or she will maintain financial support for the child, benefiting both child and custodial parent. Finally, maintaining the relationship with both parents is a protection against unexpected changes in the future. Should the custodial parent die or otherwise be unable to take care of the child, the noncustodial parent who has maintained a relationship with the child can assume the responsibility for the child's upbringing.

> *Sharon, age eight, and Brian, age four, were the focus of their parents' litigation with regard to access for almost four years following the parent's separation. There had been no disagreement that custody should remain with their mother. The parents' conflict was primarily in relation to their views of the influence of each parent's new marital partner. After months of counseling with the parents, their partners, and the children, including several months in which access was supervised by the clinician, a fragile but nonetheless functioning plan for structured access was developed. Two years later, the children's mother died of leukemia. Their father was able to assume custody and support the children's ongoing contact with their mother's parents and her partner.*

Disadvantages of Access

One must not assume that access occurs without any difficulties. Access, even when overtly unconflictual, may cause some difficulties for the child.

One difficulty is that access interferes with the child's desire and need to settle down into normal routines after the turmoil of family breakdown. Routines such as playing with friends after school or involvement in organized activities may be disrupted. Frequently the absent parent is convinced that the child's reluctance for visits is based in the custodial parent's negative view of access rather than the child's own need for normal childhood activities. In a few access disputes, it was found that the child's desire to settle down was the major, if not the only, cause of the dispute.

If either parent becomes involved in a new relationship, particularly one in which the new partner also has children from a previous union, the child may feel like an outsider in the new family unit. In a number of the Custody Project families in which access was disputed, the child's resistance to the noncustodial parent's new partner or family unit was the major factor.

Access may continuously place the child under differing sets of values and expectations in the homes of the parents. Attempting to reconcile or shift gears between these differing values and expectations can be difficult. Some children may not progress in the development of an inner identity but instead manifest an "as-if" quality. One must not underestimate a child's ability to accommodate to contradictory sets of values and expectations and emerge with a stable identity, however. Most children from intact families experience value differences to some degree between the family of origin and extended family connections.

Parents might use access as another area of conflict to pressure each other. The few minutes it takes to pick up a child can become the occasion for major conflict. The anxiety of seriously disturbed parents who maintain a symbiotic relationship with the child may be transmitted to the child. Thus, a child may remain unhappy during the visit and show serious symptoms after the visit. The disturbed parent can use the visits to pressure the other parent and to check on him or her through questioning the child, placing the child in an untenable position.

Access can be used as a weapon when money is a major area of conflict. The parent with access may refuse to pay financial support unless he or she gets the amount and quality of access demanded. Similarly, the custodial parent refuse access unless the monetary demands are met.

Finally, access can maintain the child's fantasy of parental reunion despite both parents' firm decision to end the marriage. This fantasy is stronger when neither parent is involved with another person or when the child has a good relationship with both parents. In the perception of the younger child particularly, it is evident that the child equates each parent's loving and positive relationship with the child, with the child's view that a positive relationship between the parents must ensue. The maintenance of this fantasy is undesirable because it is unrealistic, requiring much energy from the child to maintain. It is then a continuing source of distress and disappointment for the child when the fantasy does not become reality.

Development of an Access Plan

The two theoretical stances that guide our work in this area and that might appear contradictory need to be restated. One is that access is an expected occurrence following marital separation because it is a child's right. Conversely, access should not be considered the inalienable right of a parent. Presenting these statements at the beginning of work with separating parents begins an educative process particularly with those parents who are reluctant either to allow or to exercise access. There is equal likelihood of damage to children by the parent who is unreliable in exercising access as from the parent who undermines or sabotages access.

No access plan is to be perceived as permanent or as the model access plan. One aspect of the process of assisting parents to develop plans for access is to increase their ability to develop flexibility for the future. It is useful to think of access as a continuing process, reflecting an ongoing adaptation to the changing developmental needs of the child and the changing circumstances of the parents' lives. Thus, any plan that relates realistically to the child's needs and is agreeable to the parents is acceptable.

Appropriate access is determined by factors that are subject to change, including the following:

Age and the developmental needs of the child.

Wishes of the parents and the children. The greater is the congruence between both parents and children's wishes, the greater is the possibility of flexible access planning.

Conflict between the parents and/or a parent and the children, which narrows the flexibility of planning markedly.

Ability of the parents to negotiate between themselves and with the children.

Geographic locations of the parents and the demands of their employment.

Child's education and leisure-time activities.

Future changes for the parents, particularly those that occur with remarriage or major geographic moves.

To attempt to put in place a rigid access plan that can accommodate all of these factors is unrealistic. Of far greater importance is the ability of parents to negotiate with each other or to seek clinical services to assist in dispute resolution.

Guidelines with regard to access can be discussed with parents who are reasonable and relatively healthy, and these may become a basis for agreement. Four guidelines are important:

1. An access plan needs to allow predictable and frequent access by the child to the noncustodial parent.

2. A preschooler needs a more stable environment than older children. Thus frequent brief visits are preferable to day-long or overnight visits.

3. For the school age and the older child, increasing control by the child of the frequency and the duration of the visits is to be preferred. While adhering to the principle of continuous and frequent access, the child in latency or adolescent years is more mobile and thus can often undertake more responsibility in negotiating visits with the absent parent.

4. Issues relating to the care and control of the child, such as routines, health care, education, leisure-time activities, and religion, are best agreed upon jointly by the parents and supported by both of them if the child is not to be faced with conflicting expectations. Agreement on these areas by both parents and a commitment to support one another lessens the potential for the child to play one parent off against the other.

> *Bobby Grant loved his father and initially enjoyed frequent visits with him. When his father was irregular in his visiting and turned to alcohol and girlfriends, Bobby became anxious, depressed, and frightened. When his dad returned to more reliable visiting, Bobby responded by becoming a more relaxed child again.*

For parents who remain in severe conflict in the postseparation stage, such general guidelines are not helpful. If anything, the essential flexibility of these guidelines can be perceived as ambiguous, allowing for continued parental conflict. Instead a clear and rigid access plan may be required since any changes may precipitate conflict. For such parents, the following principles are useful as a guide:

1. The child resides in one home, and that is the home of the custodial parent. This is the place where the child spends most time, keeps most belongings, and from where most activities originate. The custody arrangements should clearly support the child in feeling he or she lives in that home and visits with the noncustodial parent.

2. The custodial parent carries the primary responsibility for the child's rearing. Daily routines, education, religion, health care, and leisure-time activities where possible should be discussed with the noncustodial parent but are to be decided by the custodial parent. Support of these plans during access visits is expected of the noncustodial parent.

3. The age of the child is a primary factor in planning the duration of visits, location, and frequency. The needs of the preschool child are different from those of the older child.

4. Changes in visiting arrangements arising out of changes in the child's activities or illness in either the child or one of the parents are to be expected and planned for. Visiting should disrupt the child's normal routines as little as possible. In other words, the visiting parent should adapt, insofar as possible, to the child's schedule, and not vice-versa. Mechanisms for making an unexpected change in visiting plans can be established, requiring minimal negotiation between the parents.

5. Making access visits into special occasions is to be avoided. Rather it is preferable for the parent and the child to undertake normal activities. To maintain visits as special occasions places a strain on the noncustodial parent, limits the opportunity for the development of an easy parent–child relationship, and may risk alienation of the custodial parent. The custodial parent may perceive himself or herself as carrying out the basic child-rearing responsibilities, whereas the visiting parent reaps the benefits.

When an access plan cannot be mediated, these guidelines are referred to in the written opinion forwarded to the referring lawyers or court.

Access rarely proceeds without difficulties. A child may appear upset and withdrawn following a visit or may not sleep well before or after a visit. Commonly the custodial parent assumes that such difficulties are caused by the bad influence of the visiting parent. Similarly, the visiting parent is often convinced that the child's difficulties are caused by the custodial parent who is undermining the visits. It is important for the clinician not to assume a causal relationship between visits and symptomatology. It may well be that the child is upset by the visit but that the upset is due to the change of routine rather than to any inherent problems with the visit. Also the upsets may be the result of negative attitudes of either parent. In most families, so long as the parents continue to adhere to realistic access arrangements, such behavioral responses on the part of the child disappear quickly. Premature termination of the access visit because of reported behavioral difficulties is ill advised. At times, one parent may have to live with difficulties around visits. The ideal of totally problem-free access is a goal that may be sought but not always achieved.

Techniques of Intervention in Access Disputes

The techniques of intervention in access disputes can be thought of in three phases: assessment; mediation or, if necessary, recommendation on the basis of the clinicians' opinion; and implementation. The assessment of access disputes is similar to the assessment process used in custody disputes. The basic focus is to determine whether there are major reasons for not establishing visits. The type and frequency of access rather than its basic desirability is more often the issue. While collecting assessment data, the clinician concurrently begins an educative process with both parents and children with regard to the needs of all family members as they adapt to a different life-style. In the mediation or recommendation phase, the clinician synthesizes the assessment data and formulates for the factors relating to this particular family's problems and needs with regard to access. The pros and cons of access from the point of view of the least detrimental alternative to the child are discussed.

The preferred goal in an access dispute is to assist the family in reaching agreement about an access plan. This may require from one to several sessions with the parents or long-term work with the family. Most of the Custody Project families disputing access were able to reach agreement. Over the years, three methods of intervention by the Custody Project members have evolved: clinical work with a family, supervised access, and collaboration with counsel.

The clinical work with the family is primarily educative, to learn about the importance of access for the child and his or her developmental needs. Suggestions, confrontations, and interpretations play a role as well. For example, in one case, the reluctance of the mother of a preschooler to allow the father access was based on her own pain at being left by him. Both parents were basically reasonable people, but their conflict escalated through mutual negative interactions. The clinician was able to help the wife accept her loss, reinstate access, and convince the father to resume financial support and to withdraw his application for custody in a period of three months. A follow-up after six months showed that conflict-free access was continuing. In another example, intensive clinical work lasted eighteen months and has continued on an intermittent basis when requested by the parents. In this situation, the custodial mother was a borderline personality with a history of several serious suicide attempts. The separation had occurred four years earlier; the father had remarried and had another child. The mother had not worked through the separation, the access was severely conflicted, and the child was symptomatic. The clinician arranged for the child to be in therapy with another therapist and worked with the mother, father, and his new wife. Continued counseling resulted in vastly improved access and improvement in the child and allowed time for the custodial mother to consider her child's needs. Subsequently the custody of the child was shifted to the father from the mother at her request, without further conflict.

The second method is supervised access. There are two facets in supervised access. First, the response of the child to visits with the absent parent requires observation and at times intervention by a clinician if the visits are not to be traumatic to the child. The absent parent may need education and modeling with regard to improved means of relating to the child. Second, because situations requiring supervised access include a high level of interparental conflict and resistance, it has been the practice to have the clinician initially present in the playroom with the child and the absent parent. When their play is progressing well, the clinician joins the custodial parent, who is observing the visit through a one-way mirror. The observation of the former spouse as a parenting person, with the child enjoying the visit, provides the most explicit education. Clinical intervention may be needed more with regard to the parents' anxiety about contact between them rather than in relation to the absent parent's behavior with the child. Supervised access by the clinician is time-consuming. It has not been provided for longer than a four-month period for any family. Some families have responded well and have been able to transfer from this format to supervised access by another neutral resource or to a structured access format. When access cannot evolve in one of these two ways, denial of access must be considered.

There remains a small group of families in which the conflict between the parents is so strong that no plan can be elicited from them, nor will the clinician's recommendations or a court order be accepted. The Custody Project members have at such times requested a meeting with the lawyers, the assessment findings are given in detail, the unsuccessful attempts at mediation are described, and the clinician's opinion with regard to access is made clear. In our experience, the lawyers can utilize the clinical findings with their clients and through this may achieve a solution to the access dispute other than continued litigation. Involvement of counsel has also been found helpful when the clinician has not been able to establish a therapeutic alliance with a parent. It would appear that the lawyer, perceived by his or her client as an ally, is better able to suggest a clinical recommendation, providing the lawyer understands the basis of the clinical opinion from which the recommendation is derived. If no agreed-upon plan can be achieved through the efforts of the lawyers as well, then the clinician must provide to counsel, in writing, the assessment findings and the preferred recommendation for access for use in a court proceeding. It is paramount to emphasize that access imposed or forced on unwilling parents and/or children has little chance of being beneficial.

Denial of Access

The Custody Project members believe that loss of a continuing relationship with a parent or significant extended family members as a result of separation or divorce has serious emotional and social implications for both the child and the rest of the family. Denial of access is in opposition to our basic belief that a child requires an ongoing relationship with both parents for optimal emotional and social growth. Despite this strong commitment, denial of access was recommended in 4 percent of the families in the project's population. A review of these families suggests that denial of access was based on one or more of the following reasons:

1. The pathological behavior of the visiting parent caused severe distress for the child. Such behavior included a high risk of violence toward the child and/or the custodial parent; a continuing risk of child abduction; habitually disruptive behavior by the visiting parent because of mental illness or alcohol or drug abuse; and chronic irresponsibility on the part of the visiting parent in carrying out the access arrangement reliably.

2. Continuing severe conflict between the parents that involved the child either directly or through parental demands for the child to report to each parent about the other. The conflict may be related to various issues from the parents' past or present lives, but it is displaced onto the conflict about access.

3. Extreme rigid opposition to access by the custodial parent based on personal, cultural, or religious attitudes of that parent. In these situations, the totality of the custodial parent's rejection of the other parent results in the absent parent's becoming a nonperson, with the child having no choice but to conform to the custodial parent's attitude.

4. Intense and vehement opposition by a child to visits with the absent parent, to the degree that only physical holding of the child will maintain the child in the same room with the visiting parent.

5. The noncustodial parent applies for access following years of no contact with the child. These situations usually resulted from parental separation around the time of the child's birth, with no access sought. Subsequent access required introduction of the biological parent to the child. In some situations, this would have been disruptive to the child's adjustment and was firmly opposed by the child and the custodial parent.

The following case examples show that a combination of these reasons was evident in such situations, which led to a recommendation to the parents, counsel, and the courts that access be denied.

> *Mr. and Mrs. Gianetto had seven children ranging in age from nine to twenty-one years. The three older children were living independently; the four younger children were living in Mr. Gianetto's care with the support and supervision of the child welfare authorities. Seven years prior to the referral to the Custody Project, Mrs. Gianetto had a schizo-*

phrenic illness in which the children became incorporated into a fixed delusional system in which the sons were idealized and the daughters perceived as sluts. The four younger children had been visiting with their mother in supervised access visits in the offices of the child welfare agency. This plan had been instituted some years earlier as a means of containing the mother's inappropriate and insistent demand to see the children at their school. All four children objected to the supervised visits except for the fifteen-year-old boy, who was Mrs. Gianetto's preferred child. The children all complained, however, that their mother's behavior embarrassed them. Her verbally abusive language to her daughters was extremely upsetting to them. Denial of access was recommended. All the children, including the fifteen-year-old son, experienced relief.

The existence of mental illness by itself is not sufficient reason to deny access; rather, the risk of adverse effects of the illness on the child is the guideline.

Mr. and Mrs. Kent had divorced several years earlier. Mrs. Kent had remarried, and the four children were living with her and their stepfather. The children were ages nine to fifteen; the younger two had no memory of living with their biological father. The stepfather was actively involved with the children in their activities; the warmth of their relationship with him was evident. In contrast, Mr. Kent had been very inconsistent in visiting with the children. For two years, his whereabouts were unknown. When he resumed contact with them, the children found him rigid, distant, and uninterested in them. The eldest boy invited Mr. Kent to attend a special scouting event in which the boy was to receive an award; the younger daughter twice invited Mr. Kent to attend a school play in which she was the star. Although agreeing to attend these important events, Mr. Kent failed to appear at any of them.

Mr. Kent terminated a week of vacation with his children two days early with no forewarning to the children or their mother, who was out of town. He returned the children to a neighbor and left them there. After three years of incidents of this kind, Mrs. Kent and her husband, at the children's request, asked that access be much less frequent and be supervised. The clinical recommendation was that access be left to the discretion of the children.

Cindy, age six, had been living with her mother since the parents' separation two years earlier. The marriage had been stormy from its inception. Mrs. Turner accused her former husband of repeated physical abuse of her, which increased in severity when she refused to conform to his demand that her pregnancy with Cindy be aborted. She reported that Mr. Turner had also been abusive to Cindy. Mr. Turner denied her accusations of violence. In turn, he accused Mrs. Turner of isolating him from Cindy by talking to their child in her mother tongue, which he did not understand, and of reiterating stories about antisocial behavior in which he and his brothers had been involved in order to ensure that Cindy would be fearful of him. He stated that the cause of the marital breakdown had been Mrs. Turner's sexual frigidity.

Assessment findings indicated that mother and daughter were in a pathologically symbiotic relationship, both socially isolated except for their daily attendance at church. Mr. Turner, however, had a lengthy history of assaultive behavior, and within the interview context was labile in mood, threatening and impulsive. The treatment needs of Mrs. Turner and Cindy were seen as the priority issue; however, the possibility of future violence by Mr. Turner was high. As long as Mr. Turner's threatening presence remained in their lives, he remained a force aligning mother and daughter ever more tightly. Denial of access was recommended.

In some cases, the child refused to continue to comply with previously arranged access.

Karen's parents separated when she was two and a half. She remained with her mother, with frequent access visits with her father for the subsequent five years. Her mother remarried and left her job when Karen was age seven. For the first time in Karen's memory, her care was provided by her mother at home, with no day care by others needed. The father's reaction to the mother's remarriage was to decrease support payments for Karen. The child began refusing access visits to the point that it would have required bodily force to have her accompany her father.

Karen's motivations appeared multiple in this change in attitude toward long-established access. First, she was able to spend more time with her mother. Second, she was reflecting her mother's anger at the father for decreasing support payments. Finally, she was apprehensive about her mother's pregnancy and the change in her life that the expected child would cause. Extensive efforts were made to deal with these issues; however, Karen remained adamant in her refusal of access.

Agreement was reached among Karen's mother, her new husband, and her father that access would be terminated and that her father would maintain contact by telephone calls and attendance at school functions. A year later, access was resumed following a period of supervised access in the clinician's office.

The final example presents a case in which the absence of relationship between a child and parent was a primary factor in recommending denial of access.

Mr. and Mrs. Willis married in their teens and had two children, Robby and Sherry. The family lived with Mr. Willis's parents throughout the three years of marriage prior to Mrs. Willis's leaving the home. At the point of referral to the Custody Project, Robby was age nine and Sherry age six. The children's primary caretaker had been Mr. Willis's mother. In the six years following the separation, Mrs. Willis's visits with the children had been infrequent, with none in the previous two years. Mrs. Willis did not feel accepted by her former husband's family and made attempts to visit the children at their school. Robby expressed fear that Mrs. Willis would try to take him away from home forever. Sherry did not know her mother. On the basis of this lack of relationship between Mrs. Willis and her daughter and Robby's fearfulness, the recommendation was made that access be denied.

Although courts and clinicians may be reluctant to support denial of access, some extreme circumstances warrant this on the basis of the child's psychological and physical protection. Clinicians continue to struggle with a number of concerns regarding denial of access. These include the theoretical uncertainty about the nature of personality development should a child's relationship with one parent be arbitrarily terminated and the parameters that are related to the stage of the child's development. The long-term consequences of denial of access are not known. An analogy may be drawn from adoption studies that describe a need that surfaces in adolescent adoptees to seek their roots and resolve their identity. Thus denial of access may be appropriate at one stage in the child's life but not in another.

It may be argued that even a negative parental relationship is preferable to no relationship with that parent. The extreme tension provoked in the cases presented far exceeds the bounds of a negative relationship. In each case, the child's physical and/or emotional development was in jeopardy.

Summary

The resolution of an access dispute is more complex and demanding than a custody dispute, and there is greater potential for damage to the children because the unresolved parental conflict may continue endlessly. We believe that access is the child's right and should be planned with the child's needs paramount. Alternatives for access planning should be selected on the basis of the realities of the child's age and stage of development and the parents' life circumstances. These alternatives can usually be developed by the family members, over time, with assistance from an objective mental health professional.

Epilogue

The Grants

Referral to the Custody Project was made by the parents' lawyers at the firm request of the court. In the initial meeting with counsel, Mr. Grant's lawyer emphasized his position that the matter should go to trial and that he would so advise his client. In his opinion, no court would deny access by a father to his son in a situation in which the father had had continuous contact throughout the child's life. The lawyer viewed the abduction of Bobby by his father lightly and had little interest in the quality of the access visits in the past. Mrs. Grant's lawyer stated clearly his client's view that further access should be denied but was prepared to consider a mediated solution provided that Bobby's physical and emotional safety could be protected and that Mrs. Grant could have confidence in that.

In the initial clinical interviews, Bobby was frightened and somewhat depressed and anxious. He described his abduction by his father and the subsequent two weeks in the home of people previously unknown to him as "bad" and "scary." Not without personal resources, this five year old had made two abortive attempts to seek help: he had tried to telephone his mother but apparently dialed incorrectly, and he had told a policeman (actually a security guard in the housing development in which his father's friends lived) about his troubles. He had been deeply worried that his mother and paternal grandparents would be crying and upset.

Mrs. Grant recognized that Bobby remained attached to his father despite the adverse impact of recent access visits and the abduction. In her view, her former husband's behavior had been strongly influenced by his new marital partner, whom she perceived as resenting Mr. Grant's interest in Bobby. Clinical observations of Mr. Grant and his partner supported this view.

With the agreement of Bobby, both parents, and their lawyers, four access visits supervised by the clinician were undertaken as part of the assessment process. The plan was that Bobby would be brought to the visits by either his maternal or paternal grandparents and that the visit would be with Mr. Grant and his new partner. For two visits, Mr. Grant and his partner did not appear or make any attempt to cancel the appointments. In the remaining two visits, Mr. Grant demonstrated clearly that he was torn between his affection for Bobby and his need to please his new partner. In individual interviews he recognized that his own ambivalence resulted in insensitivity to Bobby's needs. His partner remained adamant that Bobby was spoiled and overdemanding of his father's attention; equally, she rejected any plan for Mr. Grant to maintain contact with Bobby in the home of his parents.

Efforts to mediate were unsuccessful. To the parents and counsel, the recommendation was made that access by Mr. Grant to Bobby be terminated but that contact between Bobby and his father's parents be maintained through the arrangements made between them and the maternal grandparents, who continued to provide day care for Bobby. Mr. Grant's impulsivity and emotional immaturity and his partner's negative attitude to Bobby were also factors in the denial of access recommendation.

Subsequently a court order was made following this recommendation. Bobby and his mother were seen for some months by the clinician, the focus of treatment being resolution of Bobby's mourning for his father.

The Gerrards

In the initial meeting with both parents' lawyers, the extraordinary tension felt by all family members in the cohabiting but separate and apart arrangement was recognized. The situation was so volatile that both lawyers were receiving calls from their clients almost daily. The clinician doubted that an effective mediation-assessment process could be carried out in this context. Counsel were able to clarify the emotional, financial, and legal problems in which the arrangement had been based. Pending approval of their clients, counsel agreed that a written agreement could be drafted without prejudice to either parent in which one parent, likely Mr. Gerrard, would leave the matrimonial home temporarily, and a liberal access arrangement would be maintained for the absent parent either within the matrimonial home but in the absence of the other parent or outside the home.

For the ensuing two months, Mrs. Gerrard and the children remained in the home. On weekends Mrs. Gerrard stayed with her parents, while Mr. Gerrard stayed in the matrimonial home with the children. During the week Mr. Gerrard saw the children at least once, but the children were reluctant to have additional visits with him unless his partner were absent.

Once physical separation occurred, Mrs. Gerrard's parenting skills became more evident in practical and emotional care of the children. Mr. Gerrard's focus remained primarily on the children's academic achievement. His rigid and authoritarian manner altered minimally and was particularly noticeable in his premature demand for the children to be demonstratively affectionate with his new partner, Lynn.

A significant step was made during a family interview when the parents heard the children's view that although they wanted to remain in their current neighborhood and school area, they had only painful memories of the family home and hoped that the parents' separation would result in a move to a new home or apartment in the same district. The emotional aspects of the battle over the matrimonial home decreased markedly. Both parents were nonplussed in the face of the children's primary emphasis on remaining together. Neither parent had recognized the extent to which the children had turned for support to one another rather than to a parent. Both needed time and assistance in considering each child's response to the previous marital conflict, the father's decision to seek a divorce, and his new marital partner. In joint interviews, the parents' ability to share their observations of each child's behavior and adjustment was strengthened. Agreement was reached by the parents that the children remain together in their mother's care, with liberal access by Mr. Gerrard to the children. The older children were encouraged to arrange visits with their father, and they in turn undertook to facilitate transportation of the younger children to their father's home. Individual work was undertaken with Mr. Gerrard, and subsequently with his partner, with regard to the children's accommodation to his new relationship. In effect, a shared parenting plan was developed, although in the minutes of settlement, it was agreed that Mrs. Gerrard would have sole custody of the children. A year later, both parents supported a joint custody plan, and this was so ordered by the court.

Credo

IT IS THE AUTHORS' BELIEF THAT:

• At the point of family breakdown, parents hold equal responsibility for planning for their children's future.

• Planning for the children's custody and access arrangements must place the children's needs paramount.

• The most effective custody and access plan is one that is designed by the family members.

• Children of separated and divorced parents have a right to have their own wishes heard about their futures.

• It is each child's right to have a continuing relationship with both parents, siblings, and extended family members.

• It is the obligation of the legal and mental health professionals to coordinate their services to facilitate the productive use of their services by families disputing custody and access plans for the children.

• A continuum of techniques of intervention is required to meet the needs of separating and divorcing families, flexibly utilized by skilled mental health professionals according to the needs and capabilities of the individual family.

Appendix A
Referral Package

CUSTODY PROJECT
DEPARTMENT OF PSYCHIATRY
UNIVERSITY OF TORONTO

EIGHT FLOOR
950 YONGE STREET
TORONTO, CANADA
M4W 2J4
(416) 924-5431

Thank you for your enquiry regarding our service. The Custody Project was established by the Division of Child Psychiatry of the Department of Psychiatry, University of Toronto, in order to provide clinical assessment and recommendations for families involved in child custody and access litigation. Our clinicians are psychiatrists, psychologists, and social workers holding positions within the University's psychiatric network and all have considerable experience dealing with complicated family disputes. Administration of the Project is carried out at the Family Court Clinic of the Clarke Institute of Psychiatry where I am a staff psychiatrist.

The Project developed in response to a need for clinical service and for the development of knowledge and techniques in the area of custody and access disputes. Therefore our goals are to make service available to Courts and counsel and to use our accumulated experience and research data to enlarge our knowledge in family and marital pathology, child development, and related areas. Project members are frequently asked to provide training for others and to make professional presentations for those less experienced in the field. We have also attempted to work closely with the Courts and the Bar in developing procedures which are clinically useful to families while also providing professional opinion and recommendations.

In accordance with contemporary principles in child and family psychiatry, we become involved in custody and access disputes only if all family members are available for participation.

/...2

Page Two
Re: Custody Project

Therefore it is necessary to see both parents, the children, and anyone else who may play a significant role in the situation. We believe that evaluation of only one side of the dispute must be biased and therefore inadequate. Therefore we will begin an assessment only if all parties agree to be involved.

In situations where families are fragmenting and custody and access arrangements must be developed, there are no perfect solutions but we hope to find those which are least damaging. Our clinicians attempt to consider a range of solutions, generated by discussion with all parties. These are then evaluated relative to each other.

Our procedures usually include the following: individual and joint interviews with all of the children and adults involved, collection of relevant medical, psychiatric, and social information, and consultation with counsel. The process includes discussion and educative efforts with respect to the effects of marital separation. Following the initial interviews the clinician usually tries to explore the possibility of resolving the dispute. Such attempts will be ''open'' and information obtained may be revealed in a subsequent assessment report. We do not undertake ''closed mediation'' in which it is agreed that the content of the sessions will not be revealed to counsel or the Court. Should our efforts to find a solution be unsuccessful, the clinician will discuss the alternative solutions which are being proposed and will offer an opinion in order to assist counsel and the Court.

As you are aware, these difficult disputes are time-consuming for clinicians as well as for counsel. When a referral has been completed it can usually begin within two to four weeks. When the initial interviews begin, the process described above can take from one to three months depending on a variety of factors. It is our experience that parents can sometimes begin to think more flexibly about their children's situation and needs as we work with them over a period of weeks.

/...3

Page Three
Re: Custody Project

As stated earlier our clinicians are psychiatrists, social
workers and psychologists. Most commonly a case is looked after
by one clinician but at times it may be felt advisable to
recruit a colleague to share the work. In addition, a member of
one discipline may be used as a consultant by a member of
another discipline, e.g., a psychologist providing testing for
a social worker or psychiatrist. If this is necessary, counsel
will be notified. Cases are usually assigned by the Project
Administrator in accordance with the availability of any of the
Project members to take on a new case.

The clinician is expected to carry out the appropriate clinical
work, to be available for meetings with counsel, and to attend
Court if requested. Written reports will include a summary of
the clinician's activities in the case, relevant historical
material and clinical observations in regard to the parties,
discusssion of the various possible solutions to the dispute,
and any specific recommendations which the clinician may wish
to make.

The fees for this work vary from $45.00 to $125.00 per hour.
Project members usually bill in accordance with the fee
schedule of their respective professional associations. The
clinician to whom your case is assigned will contact you to
negotiate fees and too clarify any ambiguities in the case
before proceeding to see the clients. The total time to carry
out this work, including the report, usually comes to between
15 to 20 hours, but this estimate is sometimes exceeded.
Clinicians are prepared to inform counsel if the assessment is
likely to be prolonged and to create additional expense.

Generally the fees are shared equally by both parties but at
times a larger portion of the fee may be paid by one party.

In addition to professional fees we require an administrative
fee of $100 payable to the ''Custody Project'' at the above
address. This fee is usually shared equally by both parties.
The fee should accompany your referral letter and referral

/...4

Page Four
Re: Custody Project

forms (see attached). Should your request for assessment be
subsequently withdrawn, the fee for administration is not
refundable. We also require a written undertaking with respect
to responsibility for payment of professional fees by counsel.
Should there be a change in counsel, the assessment will be
stopped until consent and undertaking from the new counsel have
been received by the Project Administrator.

Clinicians usually submit monthly accounts to counsel during
the course of the assessment. Hourly rates are charged for
review of written material, telephone consultation, and report
writing as well as for clinical sessions. It is expected that
your undertaking will cover any requests for attendance at
Court, to be paid at the clinician's hourly rate. This is also
true for legally aided cases.

In making the following referral, please send the following:

1. A letter outlining problems, relevant background, and an
undertaking by counsel with respect to fees. Please advise
which legislation is involved, e.g. Children's Law Reform Act,
Divorce Act. Copies of this letter should be sent to counsel for
all parties.

2. Completed referral forms.

3. A cheque payable to the Custody Project for your portion of
the Administrative Fee.

Should you have further questions, please contact Ms. Jeanette
deLevie, Project Administrator.

Yours truly,

Eric Hood, M.B., Ch.B., F.R.C.P.(C)
Director, Custody Project
Assistant Professor
Department of Psychiatry
University of Toronto

:hw

REFERRAL TO CUSTODY PROJECT

When making a referral to the Custody Project, please make sure that you have included the following:

1. Referral Letter

2. Referral Form

3. Parent Questionnaires

4. Administrative fee of $100 made payable to the ''Custody Project'' (can be shared).

5. Undertaking by counsel for payment of assessment fees.

We are unable to proceed with a case until the above have been received from counsel.

Should you have any questions please contact Ms. Jeanette deLevie, at 924-5431.

CUSTODY PROJECT
DEPARTMENT OF PSYCHIATRY
UNIVERSITY OF TORONTO

REFERRAL DATE: _____

NAMES OF PARENTS (GUARDIANS)

1. _____ Relationship
    FIRST   MIDDLE   LAST   to Child _____

    ADDRESS _____ PHONE NUMBER: _____

Relationship

2. _____ to Child _____

    ADDRESS _____ PHONE NUMBER:

_____

Relationship

3. _____ to Child _____
    FIRST   MIDDLE   LAST

    ADDRESS _____ PHONE NUMBER: _____

CHILDREN INVOLVED

	NAME	AGE	SEX	IN WHOSE CARE	LEGAL CUSTODIAN
1.					
2.					
3.					
4.					
5.					
7.					

COUNSEL _____

1. _____ PHONE: _____

   _____

2. _____ PHONE: _____

   Representing _____

3. _____ PHONE: _____

   Representing _____

____COURT_____   JUDGE _____

Referral requested by _____

Date set for next hearing _____

The issue before the court is _____

_____

_____

_____

_____

Other resources previously or presently involved:

C.A.S. _____ Contact Person _____

C.C.A.S. _____ Contact Person _____

Mental Health Service _____

Private Physician, Psychiatrist, Psychologist, etc. _____

_____

Other relevant agency (psychiatric hospital, Addiction Research
Foundation, etc.) _____

_____

_____

Please accompany this form with a letter requesting referral, and
adding relevant information regarding problem, and background and
nature of service desired.

Copies of this letter should be sent to all counsel involved.

CUSTODY PROJECT
DEPARTMENT OF PSYCHIATRY
UNIVERSITY OF TORONTO

PARENT (GUARDIAN) QUESTIONNAIRE
(please fill in circle)

DATE _____

1. Name of Parent and Guardian _____

2. Relationship to Child (Children) _____ 3. Age _____

4. Religion   (1) Protestant   (3) Jewish
               (2) Roman Catholic   (4) Other (specify)

                                             _____

5. Place of Birth (1) Canada (2) Europe (3) Other (specify) _____

6. If Canada (1) Ontario (2) Quebec (3) Western (4) Maritimes

7. Number of Years in Canada _____

8. Language(s) spoken in home   (1) English   (2) French
                                     (3) Other (specify) _____

9. Marital History:

    (1) Date(s) of Marriage(s) _____

    (2) Date(s) of Separation(s) _____

    (3) Date(s) of Divorce(s) _____

    (4) Date(s) of Death of Spouse(s) _____

    (5) Present Marital Status (a) Married (b) Single (c) Common-law

10. Do you live with child (children)? _____

11. If not give details (how long apart? access arrangements, etc.)

_____

_____

_____

_____

12. Your education (specify grade)

    (1) Primary (grades 1-8) _____

    (2) Secondary (grades 9-13) _____

    (3) Trade School or Adult Retraining _____

    (4) Community College _____

    (5) Apprenticeship _____

    (6) University _____

    (7) Other (specify) _____

13. Employment at Present _____

14. Hours of Work _____

15. If disabled or unemployed, please give details _____

_____

_____

16. Personal Annual Income

    (1) under $3,000
    (2) $3,000-$6,000
    (3) $6,000-$10,000
    (4) $10,000-$15,000
    (5) $15,000-$20,000
    (6) above $20,000

17. Serious illnesses (1) Yes (2) No Specify _____

_____

18. Serious accidents (1) Yes (2) No Specify _____

_____

19. History of psychiatric or emotional illness or disturbance _____

_____

COMMENTS _____

_____

_____

_____

_____

What are your personal objectives for the children in terms of custody, access, wardship? _____

_____

_____

_____

_____

_____

_____

_____

What do you feel are the obstacles? _____

_____

_____

_____

_____

_____

_____

Are you in agreement with this referral?   YES   NO

COMMENTS _____

_____

_____

_____

_____

_____

Appendix B
Sample Report
to Counsel

EIGHTH FLOOR
950 YONGE STREET
TORONTO, CANADA
M4W 2J4
(416) 924-5431

January 4, 1984

Ms. Mary Jones   Mr. John R. Black

Barrister & Solicitor   Barrister & Solicitor

440 Jarvis Street   555 University Avenue

Toronto, Ontario   Toronto, Ontario

Dear Ms. Jones and Mr. Black:

RE: Mr. Frank Williams

   Mrs. Elizabeth Williams

   Children: Cheryl Williams, 9 years

            Robbie Williams, 7 years

Mr. and Mrs. Williams were referred to you by the Custody
Project on August 20, 1984, for evaluation regarding their
dispute over custody of their children. In our discussion of
September 5, it was my understanding that each parent wished to
have sole custody of both children; both parents had clearly
stated their support for frequent ongoing contact between the
children and the other parent once custody had been decided. A
previous attempt to assist the parents to reach an agreement
about custody of Cheryl and Robbie had been unsuccessful; as
stated to you by telephone on October 5, I was equally unsuccessful in gaining the parents' agreement to a custody plan

that each could support. The following is a summary of my involvement with the Williams family and of my clinical findings and recommendations.

Assessor's Qualifications

I am a physician, having graduated from the University of Toronto in 1963. I received training in psychiatry and child psychiatry at Harvard Medical School and since 1970 have been a Fellow of The Royal College of Physicians of Canada, certified in psychiatry. Since that time I have been a staff psychiatrist at the Clarke Institute of Psychiatry and Assistant Professor at the University of Toronto. My experience in custody and access disputes derives from my participation in the University's Custody Project and with the Family Court Clinic of the Clarke Institute. My responsibilities include the supervision and training of staff and of psychiatric residents, and I am involved in research projects regarding custody and access disputes.

Summary of Assessment Activity

I first saw all of the family together on September 15, 1982. Mr. Williams was seen alone on four occasions (September 21, 28, November 12, and 19). Mrs Williams was seen alone three times (September 22, 29, November 16). The children were seen together and separately on October 5, with their mother on October 11, and with their father on October 18. They were again seen separately on November 30. Two meetings were held with counsel on September 25 and December 7. The children's school reports were made available to me, and I also received reports from the family physician and from another psychiatrist who had been involved with the parents.

Current Situation

When I first met the family, it was explained to me that Mrs. Williams had told her husband of her wish to separate eight months earlier. He was shocked and upset and attempted to persuade his wife to maintain the marriage, but after some months he concluded that she was serious about ending it. During the

preceding year Mr. Williams's job required him to spend
increasing amounts of time in Houston, Texas, and it was
expected by his employers that he would move to live there.
Separation became inevitable when Mrs. Williams made it clear
that she was not prepared to move to Houston but proposed to
continue living in Toronto with the children and to arrange
suitable access between the children and their father. Mr.
Williams in turn proposed that the children should move to
Houston with him and that they should have suitable access to
their mother.

Neither party left the matrimonial home, although Mr.
Williams's work took him away from home fairly often. During
the assessment period Mr. Williams lost his job and was no
longer required to move to Houston. In mid-October he decided
to move to Winnipeg where his own family lives and where he
feels he will have better business opportunities. He proposes
that the children leave Toronto and live with him near his
family.

Family Background

Mr. and Mrs. Williams described having met in 1966 while
attending University in Winnipeg. They married one year later
and lived in several places in Canada and the United States
while Mr. Williams completed his university and business
training and eventually settled in Toronto in 1973.

Father's History and Description of the Marriage

Mr. Williams, age 45, is the youngest of four children born to
immigrant parents and raised on a farm near Winnipeg. His
parents and siblings continue to live with their families in
that area. He described his early life as being happy and free
from difficulties and described all relationship within his own
family as positive and supportive.

Although Mr. Williams had felt that his marriage was
satisfactory, on looking back he now sees that it was not so
good. He says that his wife kept busy and was out of the house a
great deal of the time by being involved in arts and crafts
courses in the early years of the marriage. He states that his

wife had two affairs in the early years, and he feels that the biggest difference between the couple was in regard to their sense of priorities. Mr. Williams states that he was anxious to have a family, while his wife was reluctant and delayed having children. He talked of feeling deceived, manipulated, and rejected by his wife. Eventually Cheryl was born in 1975, and while Mr. Williams describes his wife as devoted to the baby, he complains that she was anxious to get back to work rather than to stay at home.

Although Mr. Williams saw the marriage as improved with the birth of his daughter, a recurrent issue appeared to be his wife's repeatedly wanting more freedom within the marital relationship. Mr. Williams sees his wife's wishes as selfish and irresponsible and his own priorities to be more appropriate—that is, to be responsible and committed to a traditional and conventional family life.

Mr. Williams stated that he was concerned that his wife would eventually reject the children and particularly their son just as she had rejected him. He believes that she has a poor attitude toward men and will not be able to give their son appropriate self-respect. On the other hand, he feels that she was been a good mother, but he has needed to remind her of her responsibilities. He complained that the house was often untidy and that his wife readily neglected her responsibilities.

He also expressed a belief that his wife would not be able to maintain an adequate home for the children because of lack of funds and that the only sensible alternative was for the children to go with him.

Mother's History and Account of the Marriage

Mrs. Williams, age 41, described having been born in Montreal and spent her early childhood there, the second of three children. Her father's business career made it necessary for the family to move for some years to Minneapolis and later to Toronto, and for several years now her parents have lived in Denver, Colorado. She had a good relationship with her mother but feels that her father was always distant and critical and that there was always a sense of strain between her parents. She enjoyed her relationships with her siblings and has happy

memories of schools, social activities, and sports during her
growing years in spite of the family's moves. In recent years
she has enjoyed frequent contact with her brother, who lives in
the Toronto area.

Mrs. Williams had had no serious boyfriends before meeting her
husband, whom she saw as very attractive and reliable. She had
doubts about marrying but was unable to stop the process once it
began. She states that the relationship changed quickly after
marriage and that her husband criticized her a great deal with
regard to housework. She tended at the time to see this as a
result of the stress of his university courses; however, she
later began to feel that her husband always had to assign blame
if anything went wrong and she was frequently the target. She
describes feeling overly controlled by her husband's demands,
and at times she has been frightened by his anger and unpredict-
ability. On one occasion, Mrs. Williams attempted to leave her
husband when she had become involved with another man, but the
other relationship was unsatisfactory, and she returned at her
husband's urging.

When she became pregnant with Cheryl, Mrs. Williams decided to
commit herself fully to the marriage and to being a mother. She
continued to be a full-time mother until both children were in
school, and she states that it was only after seven years of
looking after the children that she could find enough time for
other interests.

She described having taken part in organizing and leading
children's groups and special classes when her children were
ready for them. She believes that her husband, on the other
hand, always put his work first and that he was quite uninvolved
with the children for a number of years. She states that he
would rarely call home during the periods when he was away on
business. It is her belief that her husband became more
invested in his relationship with the children after the threat
of separation came to the surface. She feels that her husband
then began to spend more time at home and with the children and
states that he has described her to the children as being the
cause of the family breakup.

Mrs. Williams says that she has tried to protect the children
from knowing too much about the difficulties between their

parents and that she has tried to avoid being critical of her husband. However, she complains that her husband tells the children a good deal about details of the separation and predicts to them that she will be unable to provide adequately for them.

Development of the Children

Cheryl was born seven weeks prematurely but did well and was able to go home at three weeks. She is described as an anxious child who did not sleep easily in infancy and had difficulty when left alone. Numerous colds and ear infections created a hearing difficulty. She enjoyed the arrival of her brother and readily adapted to nursery school at three years. From a social point of view, she is described as a quiet leader who is sensitive to the needs of the underdog. Her recent report card gives above-average and outstanding marks in most areas, and it is clear from the teacher's comments that she is currently doing well in school both academically and socially. Cheryl is described as being more like her mother in that she is hesitant and reflective. Both parents feel that she relates closely to them and to her brother, although there are occasional quarrels.

Robbie was a healthy baby, although he had required resuscitation at birth. A series of ear infections during his early years caused a great deal of pain, but there are no lasting effects. He is described as a very social youngster and more bold and outgoing than his sister. The parents identified Robbie as being more like his father in character in his assertive and decisive style. His report card describes him as sensitive, energetic, imaginative, and showing a good sense of humor. All of his marks are average or above.

Medical Reports

Dr. J. Carr has been the family physician for several years but has had very little contact with Mr. Williams. He states that the children appear to receive better-than-average care from their mother, and he does not feel that she was exploiting the children in any way during the current struggle.

Dr. Margaret Moore, psychiatrist, saw the couple for five sessions following Mrs. Williams's announcement that she

wished to separate. It appeared that Mrs. Williams wished to
open up discussion about her marital relationship, but her
husband showed great anxiety as he attempted to achieve a
reconciliation. Dr. Moore felt that Mr. Williams strenuously
attempted to have her take his side, while Mrs. Williams seemed
sincere but guarded. Dr. Moore had concern that Mr. Williams
might impulsively move to Houston with the children.

No areas of agreement could be reached between the couple with
regard to separating or staying together.

Interviewing Impressions

Mr. Williams appeared to be a tense and pressured man who
attempted to relate to me in a friendly way and needed to exert
a good deal of control over the interview. His major thrust was
to present to me his wife's failings and inadequacies. However,
at times he could acknowledge that she had done well by the
children.

It was difficult for Mr. Williams to allow me to ask questions,
and instead he persisted in telling me what he wished me to
hear. He seemed unable to see the marital breakup as the
responsibility of both husband and wife and needed to repeatedly blame his wife for all of the difficulties. He presented
his plans for himself and the children as if there were no
sensible or logical alternatives, and it was difficult for him
to contemplate other options. It was my impression that Mr.
Williams found it difficult to tolerate interpretations of
situations which were not in total agreement with his own
preceptions. He also spontaneously provided diary notes and
other written material for me to read. I experienced a high
degree of pressure to agree with his planning.

Mrs. Williams was cooperative and pleasant and like her husband
readily gave a good deal of information. She was able to
describe her husband's strengths as well as his difficulties,
and she could empathize with his pain and struggles at present
as well as in earlier years. She was also able to talk thought-
fully about her children's feelings. Like her husband Mrs.
Williams appeared to need acknowledgment from me that her
thinking was valid, and she seemed to feel unsure that I could
understand that she had been a conscientious and loving parent.

She was anxious to keep me informed during the assessment about
improvements in her financial situation and to show that she
could competently provide for the children. She appeared to
feel unnecessarily threatened by her husband's allegations of
incompetence.

When Cheryl and Robbie were first seen together, they stated
that they felt unable to choose which parent to live with and
Cheryl added, ''and they don't ask us to.'' Cheryl was tearful
about the prospect of the family separation, and Robbie
admitted to some sadness too. Cheryl stated that she was ''kind
of used to'' her father's absences on business. She said that
her mother was always at home except when they were in school.
Both children were able to talk of enjoying activities with
each of their parents. During another session, I attempted to
have the children compare any advantages and drawbacks for them
of being in Houston with their father or in Toronto with their
mother, and I explored their thoughts about the following
areas:

1. Their time and involvement with their father.

2. Their time and involvement with their mother.

3. Their living accommodations.

4. Their schooling.

5. Their friends and social relationships.

6. Their extracurricular activities.

7. Their relationships with extended family members.

It was clear that the children perceived the move to Houston as
bringing many more changes in more areas of their life, whereas
living in Toronto with their mother would probably mean a
change of housing and that they could have less time and involvement with their father. When seen with their mother to
discuss possible future plans, Robbie first described a plan
which sounded very much like his father's intentions. Cheryl,
who was tearful, was not able to describe her mother's plan to
me. Mrs. Williams then attempted to explain carefully how the
marital quarrels and stress had led to her decision to separate
from her husband. She told the children that she wanted to continue looking after them.

When seen alone, Cheryl felt that Houston was less attractive for her than Toronto and said that more things were important to her here. She particularly saw a major loss in her relationship with her mother if she moved to Houston but only a moderate loss of contact with her father if he went alone to Houston. Cheryl also expressed concern that some of her father's statements about her mother were not really true. She quoted her father as having stated, ''Your mother doesn't really want you.''

When seen with their father in order to discuss possible plans, the children had little opportunity to express themselves because Mr. Williams immediately took control of the situation and lectured to the children about how he wanted things to be. He did not ask, inquire, or listen to any of the children's ideas and tended to answer for them when I raised questions. During this interview, Cheryl did not look at her father, and her facial expressions indicated discomfort and perhaps disagreement at times as her father spoke.

On this occasion when seen individually in my office, Robbie spontaneously picked up the colored pencils and drew a fairly detailed picture of his parents quarreling in the kitchen while he and Cheryl peeked around the door.

The children were seen individually for interviews on November 30, and at that time Cheryl was tearful, saying that the fighting at home between her parent was very upsetting. She stated that she did not like her father's new plan of moving them to Winnipeg and that she would prefer to stay in Toronto. She also stated that she feels that she gets along better with her mother and that she is happy with her school and her friends. She added that her mother's day care arrangements for brief periods of time before and after school are satisfactory for her, and she does not notice any change in the family life now that her mother is working full time.

In his interview, Robbie also stated a preference to be with his mother and added that his father often gets angry. He also said, ''My mother says to tell you what I want, but my father tells me what to say to you.'' Robbie also added that when the children

are quarreling and Cheryl teases him, ''I'd like her to go and
be with my father.''

Discussion and Recommendations

It appears that whether or not it was openly acknowledged, Mr.
and Mrs. Williams's marriage has been in difficulty since its
earliest days. Mr. Williams tended optimistically to hope that
he and his wife could develop a conventional pattern of family
life in accordance with his ideals. Mrs. Williams tended to
feel overwhelmed and domineered by her husband's wishes,
attempted to leave the marriage, but resolved to stick it out
when they began to have children. It is likely that her
investment of energy in raising the children and her husband's
preoccupation with his business and career may have created a
reasonable degree of distance between the couple for some
years, permitting a tolerable if unsatisfying relationship
between them. However, Mrs. Williams has gradually come to the
conclusion that she cannot continue in the marriage, while her
husband is shocked by her decision to separate. He appears to
have reacted by placing all of the blame for the failure of the
marriage on his wife to reduce his sense of loss and by mounting
an intensive campaign to persuade the children that they will
be happier and better cared for with him. Each parent describes
the idea of life without the children as intolerable, and, as
you are aware, a desperate struggle has developed.

With regard to the relationship between the children and the
parents, both children appear very attached to each parent and
find the idea of separation painful. The children have been
used to being in their mother's daily care and have also been
used to their father's being absent frequently on business.
Mrs. Williams's attitude toward the children seems to be
thoughtful, considerate, and sensitive to their feelings and
needs. Mr. Williams appears to take pride in the children and in
their achievements; however, he does not seem to be able to
encourage them to have thoughts and feelings of their own but
rather needs to impose his own wishes upon them.

With regard to the children's wishes, it was clear that they
would prefer not to have a separation. Cheryl in particular
expressed great distress at the thought of being separated from

her mother. Robbie, being younger and less able to imagine
future situations, initially seemed able to accept his father's
plans as quite possible and attractive. However, as his
father's plan to move to Winnipeg became more likely, Robbie's
became increasingly firm in stating his wish to live with his
mother.

It is my opinion that the least disruptive and damaging plan
would be for the children to be in their mother's custody where
the changes in their lives will be minimized. Since the
children are closely attached to their father, it would be
important for them to have regular access to him. If he is to
live in the Toronto area, then reasonable access visits with
him on alternate weekends would probably be appropriate.
This could be complemented by a fairly equal division of
vacation periods. If Mr. Williams is to live in Winnipeg, access
will probably be less frequent because of the distance. In that
case, a schedule should be worked out which might allow access
every one to two months either in Toronto or in Winnipeg,
depending on Mr. Williams's business schedule. Because both
children do well in school, I would not feel concerned about
their missing a few days of school each year in order to have
extended weekends with their father. Again I would suggest that
vacation periods be fairly evenly split if Mr. Williams is living
in Winnipeg.

Yours truly,

Robert P. Little, M.D., F.R.C.P.(C)
Custody Project

Bibliography

Abarbanel, A. 1979. Shared parenting after separation and divorce: A study of joint custody. *American Journal of Orthopsychiatry* 49(2):320–329.

Ahrons, C.R. 1980. Joint custody arrangements in the postdivorce family. *Journal of Divorce* 3(3):185–205.

———. 1981. The continuing coparental relationship between divorced spouses. *American Journal of Orthopsychiatry* 51(3):415–428.

Aichorn, A. 1964. *Delinquency and Child Guidance, Selected Papers.* New York: International Universities Press.

Ambert, A.M. 1980. *Divorce in Canada.* Toronto: Academic Press.

American Psychiatric Association. 1980. *Diagnostic and Statistical Manual of Mental Disorders.* 3d ed. Washington, D.C.: American Psychiatric Association.

Awad, G., and Parry, R.S. 1980. Access following marital separation. *Canadian Journal of Psychiatry* 25(5):357–365.

Bala, N., and Clarke, K.L. 1981. *The Child and the Law.* Toronto: McGraw-Hill Ryerson.

Bartz, K.W., and Witcher, W.C. 1978. When father gets custody. *Children Today* 7(5):2–6.

Benedek, E. 1972. Child custody laws: Their psychiatric implications. *American Journal of Psychiatry* 129(3):326–328.

Benedek, E.P., and Benedek, R.S. 1972. New child custody laws: Making them do what they say. *American Journal of Orthopsychiatry* 42(5):825–834.

Benedek, R.S., and Benedek, E.P. 1977. Postdivorce visitation: A child's right. *American Academy of Child Psychiatry* 16(2):256–271.

———. 1979. Joint custody: Solution or illusion? *American Journal of Psychiatry* 136(12):1540–1544.

Bloom, B.L.; White, S.W.; and Asher, S.J. 1979. Marital disruption as a stressful life event. In G. Levinger and O.C. Moles, eds., *Divorce and Separation.* New York: Basic Books.

Bowlby, J. 1973. *Attachment and Loss, II: Separation.* New York: Basic Books.

Brandwein, R.A.; Brown, C.A.; and Fox, E.M. 1974. Women and children last: The social situation of divorced mothers and their families. *Journal of Marriage and the Family* 36:498–514.

Brown, E.M. 1976. Divorce counselling. In D.H. Olson, ed., *Treating Relationships.* Lake Mills, Iowa: Graphic.

Burlingham, D. 1973. The preoedipal infant–father relationship. In R.S. Eissler, A. Freud, M. Kris, and A.J. Solnit (eds.) *The Psychoanalytic Study of the Child*. Vol. 28 New Haven: Yale University Press.

Caplan, G. and Caplan, R.B. 1967. Community psychiatry. I: Basic concepts. In A.M. Freedman, H.I. Kaplan, and H.S. Kaplan, eds., *Comprehensive Textbook of Psychiatry*. Baltimore: Williams and Wilkins.

Caplan, G.; Mason, E.; and Kaplan, D. 1973. Four studies of crisis in parents of prematures, In H. Barton and S. Barton, eds., *Children and Their Parents in Brief Therapy*. New York: Behavioral Publication.

Chang, P., and Deinard, A.S. 1982. Single-father caretakers: Demographic characteristics and adjustment processes. *American Journal of Orthopsychiatry* 52(2): 236–243.

Chasin, R., and Grunebaum, H. 1981. A model for evaluation in child custody disputes. *American Journal of Family Therapy* 9(3):43–49.

Colletta, N.D. 1979. The impact of divorce: Father absence or poverty. *Journal of Divorce* 3(1):27–35.

Coogler, O.J. 1978. *Structured Mediation in Divorce Settlements*. Lexington, Mass.: Lexington Books.

Coons, J.E., and Mnookin, R.H. 1978. Toward a theory of children's rights. In I.F.G. Baxter and M.A. Eberts, eds., *The Child and the Courts*. Toronto: Carswell Co. Ltd.

Desimone-Luis, J.; O'Mahoney, K.; and Hunt, D. 1979. Children of separation and divorce: Factors influencing adjustment. *Journal of Divorce* 3(1):37–42.

Despert, J.L. 1962. *Children of Divorce*. Garden City, N.Y.: Doubleday.

Dominic, K.T., and Schlesinger, B. 1980. Weekend fathers: Family shadows. *Journal of Divorce* 3(3):241–247.

Dorland's Illustrated Medical Dictionary. 1974. 25th ed. Philadelphia: W.B. Saunders.

Feldman, L.B. 1976. Processes of change in family therapy. *Journal of Family Counselling* 4:14–22.

Foster, H.H., and Freed, D.J. 1978. Life with father. *Family Law Quarterly* 11:331.

Gardner, R.A. 1976. *Psychotherapy with Children of Divorce*. New York: Jason Aronson.

———. 1982. *Family Evaluation in Child Custody Litigation*. Cresskill, New Jersey, Creative Therapeutics.

Gasser, R.D., and Taylor, C.M. 1976. Role adjustment of single parent fathers with dependent children. *Family Coordinator* 25:397–499.

Gersick, K.E. 1979. Fathers by choice: Divorced men who receive custody of their children. In G. Levinger and O.C. Moles, eds., *Divorce and Separation*. New York: Basic Books.

Goldstein, J.; Freud, A.; and Solnit, A.J. 1973. *Beyond the Best Interests of the Child*. New York: Free Press.

Goode, W.J. 1949. Problems in post-divorce adjustment. *American Sociological Review* 14 (June):394–401.

———. 1956. *After Divorce*. Glencoe, Ill.: Free Press.

———. 1971. Family disorganization, In R.K. Merton and R.A. Nisbet, eds., *Contemporary Social Problems*. New York: Harcourt Brace Jovanovich.

Grief, J.B. 1979. Fathers, children and joint custody. *American Journal of Orthopsychiatry* 49(2):311–319.

Group for the Advancement of Psychiatry. 1980. *Divorce, Child Custody and the Family.* New York: Mental Health Materials Center.

Haley, J. 1977. *Problem-Solving Therapy: New Strategies for Effective Family Therapy.* San Francisco: Jossey Bass.

Hansen, J.C., and Messinger, L. 1982. *Therapy with Remarriage Families.* Rockville, Md.: Aspen Systems Corporation.

Haynes, J.M. 1982. A conceptual model of the process of family mediation: Implications for training. *American Journal of Family Therapy* 10(4).

Herzog, E., and Sudia, C.E. 1970. *Boys in Fatherless Families.* Washington, D.C.: U.S. Department of Health, Education and Welfare, Office of Child Development, Children's Bureau.

———. 1973. Children in fatherless families. In B.M. Caldwell and H.N. Ricciuti, eds., *Review of Child Development Research.* Vol. 3: Child Development and Social Policy. Chicago: University of Chicago Press.

Hetherington, E.M. 1972. Effects of father absence on personality development in adolescent daughters. *Developmental Psychology* 7:313–326.

———. 1979. Divorce: A child's perspective. *American Psychology* 34:851–858.

———. 1983. Address given at Research Day in Child Psychiatry, Department of Psychiatry, University of Toronto, Toronto, Canada.

Hetherington, E.M.; Cox, M.; and Cox, R. 1976. Divorced fathers. *Family Coordinator* 25:417–428.

———. 1978. The aftermath of divorce. In J.H. Stevens, Jr., and M. Matthews, eds., *Mother–Child, Father–Child Relationships.* Washington, D.C.: National Association for the Education of Young Children.

Hoffman, L. 1981. *Foundations of Family Therapy.* New York: Basic Books.

Ilfeld, F.W.; Ilfeld, H.Z.; and Alexander, J.R. 1982. Does joint custody work? A first outlook at outcome data of relitigation. *American Journal of Psychiatry* 139(1): 62–66.

Jackson, A.M.; Warner, N.S.; Hornbein, R.; Nelson, N.; and Fortescue, E. 1980. Beyond the best interests of the child revisited: An approach to custody evaluation. *Journal of Divorce* 3(3):207–222.

Jencks, C. 1982. Divorced mothers, unite! *Psychology Today* (November):73–75.

Johnston, J.R.; Campbell, L.E.G.; and Tall, M.C. 1985. Impasses to the resolution of custody and visitation disputes. Paper presented at the meeting of the American Orthopsychiatry Association, April, Toronto, Canada.

Jordan, J.R. 1982. The use of history in family therapy: A brief. *Journal of Marital and Family Therapy* 8 (October):393–398.

Kargman, M.W.A. 1979. A court appointed child advocate (guardian ad litem) reports on her role in contested child custody cases and looks to the future. *Journal of Divorce* 3(1):77–90.

Kaslow, F.W. 1981. Divorce and Divorce Therapy. In A.S. Gurman and D.P. Kniskern, eds., *Handbook of Family Therapy.* New York: Brunner Mazel.

Kessler, S. 1975. In *The American Way of Divorce: Prescriptions for Change.* Chicago: Nelson-Hall.

Kulka, R.A., and Weingarten, H. 1979. The long term effects of parental divorce on adult adjustment. *Journal of Social Issues* 35(4):50–78.

Lamb, M.E. 1976. The role of the fathers: An overview. In M.E. Lamb, ed., *The Role of the Fathers in Child Development*. New York: John Wiley.

Lasch, C. 1979. *The Culture of Narcissism*. New York: W.W. Norton.

Levitin, T.E. 1979. Children of divorce: An introduction. *Journal of Social Issues* 35 (4):1–25.

Levy, A.M. 1978. Child custody determination—a proposed psychiatric methodology and its resultant case typology. *Journal of Psychiatry and Law* 6:189–214.

Lewis, M.B. 1974. The latency child in a custody conflict. *Journal of Child Psychiatry* 13:635–647.

Longfellow, C. 1979. Divorce in context: Its impact on children. In G. Levinger and O.C. Moles, eds., *Divorce and Separation*. New York: Basic Books.

Lowenstein, J.S., and Koopman, E.J. 1978. A comparison of the self-esteem between boys living with single-parent mothers and single-parent fathers. *Journal of Divorce* 2(2):195–208.

Lowery, C.R. 1981. Child custody decisions in divorce proceedings: A survey of judges. *Professional Psychology* 12:492–498.

Luepnitz, D.A. 1982. *Child Custody: A Study of Families after Divorce*. Lexington, Mass.: Lexington Books.

Mandanes, C. 1981. *Strategic Family Therapy*. San Francisco: Jossey Bass.

Miller, D.J. 1979. Joint Custody. *Family Law Quarterly* 13(3).

Minuchin, S., and Fishman, H.D. 1981. *Family Therapy Techniques*. Cambridge: Harvard University Press.

Money, J.; Hampson, J.G.; and Hampson, J.L. 1957. Imprinting and the establishment of gender roles. *Archives AMA of General Neurology and Psychiatry* 77: 333–536.

Nehls, N., and Morgenbesser, M. 1980. Joint custody: An exploration of the issues. *Family Process* 19(2):117–125.

Parry, R.S.; Hood, E.; and White, G. 1978. History of violence proceeding separation in 100 families involved in severe custody/access disputes. Unpublished manuscript.

Rapoport, L. 1962. The state of crisis: Some theoretical considerations. *Social Service Review* 36:22–31.

Robson, B.E. 1980. *My Parents Are Divorced Too*. New York: Everst House.

Roman, N., and Haddad, W. 1978. *The Disposable Parent: The Case for Joint Custody*. New York: Holt, Rinehart & Winston.

Rosen, R. 1977. Children of divorce: What they feel about access and other aspects of the divorce experience. *Journal of Clinical Child Psychology* 6(2):24–27.

———. 1979. Some crucial issues concerning children of divorce. *Journal of Divorce* 3(1):19–25.

Rutter, M. 1971. Parent–child separation: Psychological effects on the children. *Journal of Child Psychology and Psychiatry* 12:233–260.

Salk, L. 1978. *What Every Child Would Like Parents to Know about Divorce:* New York: Harper & Row.

Santrock, J.W. 1975. Father-absence, perceived maternal behavior and moral development in boys. *Child Development* 46:753–757.

Santrock, J.W., and Warshak, R.A. 1979. Father custody and social development in boys and girls. *Journal of Social Issues* 35(4):112–125.

Satir, V. 1977. *People Making.* Palo Alto, Calif.: Science & Behavior Books.

Smith, R.M., and Smith, C.W. 1981. Child rearing and single-parent fathers. *Family Relations* 30(3):411–417.

Solow, R.A., and Adams, P.L. 1977. Custody by agreement: Child psychiatrist as child advocate. *Journal of Psychiatry and Law* 5(1):77–100.

Spanier, G.B., and Casto, R.F. 1979. Adjustment to separation and divorce: A qualitative analysis. In G. Levinger and O.C. Moles, eds., *Divorce and Separation.* New York: Basic Books.

Spitz, R.A. 1945. Hospitalism: An inquiry into the genesis of psychiatric conditions in early childhood. *The Psychoanalytic Study of the Child,* Vol. 1, pp. 53–74. New York, International Universities Press.

Stack, C.B. 1976. Who owns the child? Divorce and child custody decisions in middle-class families. *Social Problems* 23(4):505–515.

Statistics Canada. 1983. *Divorce: Law and the Family in Canada.* Ottawa: Ministry of Supply and Services.

Steinman, S. 1981. The experience of children in a joint custody arrangement: A report of a study. *American Journal of Orthopsychiatry* 51(3):403–414.

Stoller, Robert J. 1968. *Sex and Gender: On the Development of Masculinity and Femininity.* New York: Science House.

Tessman, L.H. 1978. *Children of Parting Parents.* New York: Jason Aronson.

Thomas, S.P. 1982. After divorce: Personality factors related to the process of adjustment. *Journal of Divorce* 5:19–36.

Toronto Conciliation Project Final Report. 1980. Toronto: Ministry of the Attorney General of Ontario.

Tuckman, J., and Regan, R.A. 1966. Intactness of the home and behavioural problems in children. *Journal of Child Psychology and Psychiatry* 7:225–233.

Wallerstein, J.S., and Kelly, J.B. 1980. *Surviving the Break-up: How Children and Parents Cope with Divorce.* New York: Basic Books.

Warner, N.S., and Elliott, C.J. 1979. Problems of the interpretive phase of divorce-custody valuations. *Journal of Divorce* 2(4):371–382.

Watson, M.A. 1981. Custody alternatives: Defining the best interests of the children. *Family Relations* 30(3):474–479.

Weiss, R.S. 1975. *Marital Separation.* New York: Basic Books.

———. 1979a. The emotional impact of separation. In G. Levinger and O.C. Moles, eds., *Divorce and Separation.* New York: Basic Books.

———. 1979b. Issues in the adjudication of custody when parents separate. In G. Levinger and O.C. Moles, eds., *Divorce and Separation.* New York: Basic Books.

Weitzman, L.J., and Dixon, R.G. 1979. Child custody awards: Legal standards and empirical patterns for child custody, support and visitation after divorce. *UCD Law Review* 12.

Westman, J.C. 1971. The psychiatrist and child custody contests. *American Journal of Psychiatry* 127:1687–1688.

Westman, J.C., and Lord, G.R. 1980. Model for a child psychiatry custody study. *Journal of Psychiatry and Law* 8:253–269.

Words and Phrases. 1968. St. Paul: West Publishing.

Indexes

Subject Index

Author Index

About the Contributors

George Anis Awad, M.D., F.R.C.P.(C) is the director of the Family Court Clinic, Clarke Institute of Psychiatry, and associate professor of psychiatry, University of Toronto. His training has included medical school in Beirut, Lebanon, in 1968, adult psychiatry in Rochester, New York, from 1968 to 1971, child psychiatry in Ann Arbor, Michigan, from 1971 to 1973, and psychoanalysis in Toronto from 1974 to 1979. His publications are in the areas of custody and access disputes, adolescent psychotherapy, and juvenile delinquency.

Simon Kreindler, M.D. F.R.C.P.(C) trained in medicine at McGill University, Montreal (1965), and in psychiatry at the Menninger School of Psychiatry, Topeka, Kansas (1971). He is an assistant professor of psychiatry, University of Toronto, and staff psychiatrist and psychiatric consultant to Child Abuse Program, Hospital for Sick Children, Toronto. He has a private practice in child and adult psychiatry.

James C. MacDonald, Q.C., is a partner in Messrs. MacDonald & Ferrier, a Toronto law firm, which restricts its practice to family law. He is the founding chairman of the National Family Law Section of the Canadian Bar Association and president of the Family Mediation Service of Ontario. He has been chief lecturer in family law in the Bar Admission Course in Ontario and director of legal education in the province for the Law Society of Upper Canada. He has taken part in numerous continuing education programs in family law. His major writing is as co-author of *Canadian Divorce Law and Practice,* and *Law and Practice under the Family Law Reform Act of Ontario,* both published by the Carswell Company Ltd.

Robert J. Simmons, M.D., F.R.C.P.(C) graduated in medicine at University of Ottawa in 1962 and completed his training in child psychiatry at the University of Cincinnati in 1969. He is an assistant professor of psychiatry, University of Toronto, and director of the Psychiatric Crisis Team at the Hospital for Sick Children where he is also consultant to the cystic fibrosis service. In 1983 he made an extended visit to China as a consultant in child psychiatry.

About the Editors

Elsa A. Broder, M.D., F.R.C.P.(C) trained in medicine at the University of Toronto and in general and child psychiatry in Toronto, Ann Arbor, Michigan, and London, England. Since then she has been on the staff of C.M. Hincks Treatment Centre, teaching and practicing in family and child psychiatry, with a special interest in family therapy. She chairs the committee of Family and Marital Therapy Teachers of the Department of Psychiatry and consults to juvenile probation officers and to their foster care treatment program. She is a founding member of the Custody Project and has published and made numerous presentations on the topic.

Eric Hood, M.B., Ch.B., F.R.C.P.(C) trained in medicine at the University of Glasgow (1964) and in psychiatry at the University of Toronto (1973). He is director of the Custody Project and assistant professor of Psychiatry, University of Toronto. Since 1973 he has been a staff psychiatrist at the Family Court Clinic, Clarke Institute of Psychiatry, and since 1983 director of the institute's Baffin Consultation Service to the Eastern Canadian Arctic. His university responsibilities include the organization of academic teaching in child psychiatry and his research and publications also include assessment and classification of childhood disorders.

Ruth S. Parry, M.S.W., C.S.W., director of the Family Court Clinic of the Clarke Institute of Psychiatry, and coordinator of the Custody Project of the University of Toronto from 1977 to 1984, is presently director of treatment services, Kinark Child and Family Services, a childrens' mental health service. She has many publications in the areas of custody and access evaluation and mediation, and in child mistreatment. She has lectured widely, to students in social work, law, psychiatry, psychology, nursing, and education.

Elisabeth B. Saunders, Ed.D., is a staff psychologist at the Family Court Clinic, Clarke Institute of Psychiatry; lecturer, Department of Psychiatry, University of Toronto; and member of the Custody Project. She obtained a masters degree in psychology from Hebrew University, Jerusalem, in 1976 and a doctoral degree in developmental psychology from the Graduate School of Education, Harvard University, in 1979. She has obtained clinical training in child psychology at the Judge Baker Guidance Center in Boston. Her publications are in the areas of parent–child relationships and delinquency.

Elizabeth A.G. Schmitt, M.D., F.R.C.P.(C) trained in medicine (1964) and child psychiatry (1976) at the University of Toronto. In addition to maintaining private practice, she works and teaches at the Hospital for Sick Children with the Psychiatric Crisis Team. She is a lecturer in the Department of Psychiatry, University of Toronto, and a member of the Custody Project since 1977.